HOW TO SURVIVE A TOXIC WORKSPACE

20 Difficult Personalities at Work

Susan Howard

TABLE OF CONTENTS

WHY DID I WRITE THIS BOOK? 3

INTRODUCTION 5

EFFECTIVE COMMUNICATION WITH DIFFICULT WORKPLACE PERSONALITIES 8

GENERAL TIPS FOR EFFECTIVE COMMUNICATION WITH DIFFICULT WORKPLACE PERSONALITIES 11

15 TOXIC EMPLOYEE TYPES 14

The Gossiper 14

The Blamer 17

The Flyer 20

The Work Shirker 23

The Competitor 26

The Paranoid 29

The Control Freak 32

The Pessimist 35

The Narcissistic Personality 38

The Hisser 42

The Einstein Type 45

The Victim 48

The Psychopath 51

The Quiet Type 54

The Instigator 57

5 TOXIC BOSSES 60

The Inexperienced Boss 60

The Invisible Boss 63

Micromanager 66

Negative Boss 69

The Workaholic Boss 72

TOXIC PERSONALITIES AS ASSETS IN THE WORKPLACE 75

CONCLUSION 78

ONE LAST THING 81

Why did I write this book?

I am a lucky person. My workspace is almost ideal – I have nice colleagues and a great boss. I do not wake up in the morning and dread going into a toxic workplace that day. I have the same feeling when I am going to the office in the morning as when I am going back home. However, I am the exception. Many friends and people I know are not happy at their workspace. Yes, some of them do exaggerate in their assessment of their colleagues or boss, but quite often they don't know how to deal with difficult personalities.

I wrote this book to show that dealing with difficult personalities is not impossible – quite the opposite. We are all different, and quite often we can even be a difficult person for someone else without realizing it.

"It was so difficult for me to work with you for the first several weeks," one of my former colleagues told me. *"I was trying to read between lines every time you told me something. However, it was impossible, and I was frustrated, especially because I am good at understanding what other people want, even if they don't say it directly. After two months, I realized that you are simply direct; you don't leave anything between the lines. Now I know, but that period of communication with you was so difficult for me."*

One of my friends is suffering because of her boss's constant micromanaging, while her closest colleague is a typical example of a competitor personality.

Introduction

No one can survive in this competitive global environment without working as an employee or being an entrepreneur. An average full-time worker spends more time at work and with his coworkers than with his or her own family and friends. Therefore, harmony between coworkers is imperative. In addition, the importance of having a good boss cannot be overstated. However, we all know that this is often far from reality, and all of us deal with some difficult personalities.

It cannot be overstated how essential a conducive and healthy workplace environment is for both the employees and employers of an organization. A toxic work environment can not only affect the quality of the work output but can also lead to anxiety and depression and ruin one's overall quality of life. Taking this a step further, a hostile work environment can hurt one's morale, self-esteem and confidence along with negative physical implications on the body. Some potential physical ramifications of an unhealthy and hostile workplace environment are various cardiovascular diseases, hypertension, and other fatal and chronic health conditions.

Disagreements, misunderstandings and general difficulties in communication are a common workplace feature, but persistent and pervasive minor stresses are very hazardous for the long-term sanity and productivity of employees at the workplace. There is a difference between minor disagreements and communication glitches, and workplace problems that occur on a regular basis at the workplace. Routine skirmishes and scuffles create a stressful atmosphere and can completely ruin the efficiency of workers and the company's performance in general. How can this situation be brought under control? How can a harmonious ambience be maintained in the workplace? How are you dealing with these situations? Do you have enough knowledge to work with all those difficult personalities?

In the modern workplace, employees of different ethnicities, sexual orientations, education levels, socioeconomic backgrounds and personalities come together to form a holistic team. Companies embrace this diversity and have incorporated it into their company policies. Workplace diversity and differences in employees' personalities are generally healthy for both the employees and management. Every company's business unit requires a mix of different personalities that work together to foster a harmonious work environment. That sounds nice, but do you know of a company where everything is perfect? Google? Amazon? The small bakery on the corner? Your favorite restaurant? Think again. Nothing is perfect.

An inclusive and diverse workforce helps organizations in a variety of ways. Some of the benefits that companies incur when hiring a diverse workforce are increased productivity and greater creativity and innovation. Taking this a step further, the company gains a larger talent pool with an increased skillset, and the firm acquires positive employer branding. Apart from this, due to the diversity of the workforce, there is an improved understanding of the company's customer base. Consequently, businesses also see lower turnover rates, more retention and happier employees in comparison to businesses that do not value an inclusive and diverse workplace environment. The most profitable companies are those that foster an inclusive workplace in which diversity and individual differences are valued and leveraged in an effort to achieve the company's objectives. However, many employees and bosses are difficult to associate with and communicate with on a day-to-day basis at work. These individuals are categorized into various personality types by many experts according to their specific character traits. Some of these categories include narcissistic and pessimistic employees; some other difficult personalities may include the victim, the gossiper, the control freak, the paranoid employee and the psychopathic personality.

Effective Communication with Difficult Workplace Personalities

Individuals settle in their career based not just on their education, skillset, experience and intelligence. They gravitate toward different types of jobs on the basis of their personalities, cognitive styles and temperaments. All of us possess different personality traits. However, some people possess personalities that are difficult to deal with and can be a major cause of trouble when associating with them.

Difficult workplace personalities can negatively affect the welfare of individual employees as well as entire organizations. On the other hand, even in the absence of difficult and problematic personalities, personality styles that find it hard to work well together can lead to skirmishes and conflicts.

Different personality and character traits affect and powerfully influence human relations, both at home and in the workplace. In workplace situations, one cannot simply avoid a hostile or badly behaved boss. In a similar way, difficult employees and coworkers with longstanding behaviors and belief patterns that are maladaptive, rigid and cause distress to people are not pleasant company either. However, we all have our way of dealing with conflict in both our personal and professional relationships. Dealing with these dynamics is crucial to the success or failure of personal and career associations.

Generally, when confronted with personality quirks and oddities in the office, the wise thing to do is to maintain one's composure and be patient and tolerant. However, dealing with challenging personalities on a regular basis is not a cake walk.

Not all difficult individuals need to be dealt with through direct confrontation. There are work situations in which you should think twice before having a full-blown confrontation with a coworker or a boss. For instance, to derive certain benefits, it is sometimes critical to put up with a particular employee and tolerate the untoward behavior by not taking things personally. One example would be an annoyingly loud and rude coworker who is generally disliked by most coworkers but is providing great analysis for the current project that the team is working on. In this instance, it is wise to endure the coworker's quirks and offensive behavior with patience until the analysis and the work has been done.

In addition, it is important to remember that difficult personality types are just human, and they also have positive traits that may not be as obvious and. With a little effort, these strengths can be discovered and nurtured to the company's advantage, adding to the general well-being of the employees. It is essential to focus on the strengths of the employees and compliment them when they deserve it.

Furthermore, there are two fundamental aspects of every relationship and communication situation. One is the relationship that one individual has with the other person, and the other is the issue that is being discussed. Any good communicator knows how to separate and detach the person from the issue. This is accomplished by being easygoing on the person and firm on the issue. The ultimate aim in following this tactic is to make the employee comfortable enough to clearly communicate the problem. It is also beneficial to know the personality quirks that are affecting other employees due to the behavior of the employee. Conversely, taking a hard look at the issue and using problem-solving abilities to find a resolution is the best way to go. Being aggressive and rude with difficult personality types will get you nowhere and will only have major negative consequences.

One of the strategies to disarm and neutralize unreasonable and difficult behavior is the use of humor. It has proven to be a very effective and powerful tool for conflict resolution. When properly used, humor can defuse and deactivate problematic behavior, shine light on the truth and display superior disposition. Everyone who knows me will confirm that this is my favorite tool when working with difficult and not-so-nice people. Yes, I agree that we all have a different sense of humor, but this strategy can be fruitful even with the most difficult people. At the end of the day, I have nothing to lose by trying to be funny at certain times.

On the other hand, difficult personality types who spin out of control and fly off the handle need to be dealt with more rationally, and with a firmer approach. One potential tactic is to assert the consequences of the behavior of these personality trait types. One of the most important skills to incorporate in the workplace is the ability to identify and assert consequences. This is imperative when standing down a problematic employee. When properly articulated by a boss or senior management member, this approach compels the employee to shift his or her behavior from destructive to collaborative. Another strategy that can be employed by the senior management of an organization is to enforce employee etiquette terms and conditions at all times. Taking this a step further, it can also be incorporated into company policies and be made part of the corporate culture. Any violation of company etiquette or disrespect to another employee must be dealt with firmly.

There are many benefits, both for the employees and the organization, of effectively dealing with unreasonable and difficult people. On the other hand, when problematic employees and bosses are not dealt with appropriately, it can have huge negative ramifications and lead to loss of productivity. It will have an adverse effect not only on the employees but on the company as a whole. Difficult personalities may not be easy to change. However, they can be accommodated reasonably and may eventually settle into their own comfortable niche in an organization. It is essential for the management of companies to play to the strengths of these personality types and make efforts to minimize their interpersonal and job-related weaknesses. In the upcoming chapters of the book, we will explore how to deal with each difficult and problematic personality trait type.

From my personal experience, the key step is to recognize some difficult personalities and admit the impact of their behavior on you, others and the work process. However, marking a colleague as "difficult" is not enough. You need to find your modus vivendi and find a way to work with people you might dislike.

General Tips for Effective Communication with Difficult Workplace Personalities

The first thing to remember is that we are all human, and we all have bad days when life does not seem to be a bed of roses. It is in these tricky and annoying times that we need to pause, take a deep breath, and gather the patience and optimism to believe that things will change for the better and this will pass too. It's a good idea to avoid knee-jerk, immediate responses to any bad situation. People commonly take their emotional baggage from home into the workplace and vice versa. This often leads to people being less courteous and well-behaved with other people at work or home than they ordinarily would be. Therefore, it is advisable to not mix the stresses of home and the workplace.

As workers in various organizations, we all can individually and collectively change the dynamics and the forces that are negatively affecting the workplace. How do you generally describe a difficult personality? They are just not comfortable to be around. They make it obvious with their unique behaviors, which might range from being loud, uncourteous, dominating or critical, to being totally obnoxious. Problematic people come in every imaginable variety. Some are very bad listeners and are constantly talking (to be honest, I am not the perfect listener in some situations, and I am working hard to change this). There are others who must always have the last word and be the ones who conclude the show. Furthermore, some associates fail to keep commitments and meet deadlines. Yet others criticize anything and everything and are very nit-picky. Quite a few are indecisive, uncertain, irresolute and are constantly vacillating. Difficult coworkers compete with you for power, privilege and the spotlight; some go way too far in courting the boss's positive opinion—to your detriment.

In addition, dealing with these toxic personality types can get extremely challenging when they are surreptitiously and slyly criticizing you, attacking you and being aggressive towards you, or undermining your professional input. The prudent way to solve interpersonal problems is to have a private, heart-to-heart conversation with the person who is causing the discomfort or is in any way hurting and affecting your quality of work and making your life difficult for no substantive reason. Get in touch with and approach the person for a private discussion. Talk to the coworker about what you are experiencing. Maintain a communication style that focuses on your experience of the situation rather than on criticizing or condemning the other person. This can be done by explaining to your coworker the impact of their actions on you. Eventually, attempt to reach an agreement about constructive, positive and supportive actions going forward and make space for future discussions if the behavior does not change.

From my personal experience, it is not possible to have a private discussion any time you feel that you have a problem with a colleague's behavior. You must find the proper moment, when you are in the mood to explain the issue in a nice way and when you presume the person is open to listening. Trying to do this in a moment when one or both of you are in the middle of a big project or under stress will not have good results.

In some instances when this direct, frontal and head-on approach to take care of a difficult situation does not show results, then the next best alternative is to approach management or your immediate supervisor. It has to be noted that when seeking help from superiors, you need valid evidence to prove your point. Apart from this, when dealing with toxic coworkers in dysfunctional workplaces, peers who might be experiencing similar issues with the person in question would be added help to take care of the situation. Thus, it is prudent to figure out who the other victims are and include them in the pursuit of harmony and sanity at work. This provides added weight when pressuring management to find a resolution to the problem and the problematic personality. More employees addressing their concerns is essential, since managers tend to ignore or dismiss issues between coworkers if it does not directly affect management. They fail to see the ultimate consequences of the behavior of the toxic personality on the productivity of the other employees and the company as a whole. Taking this a step further, extremely difficult personality types, like the psychopath, have to be referred to healthcare professionals.

However, looking at the situation from a more positive perspective, most of the character traits of these difficult personalities can be used in productive ways at the workplace. For instance, the Einstein type individual with lots of ingenious and innovative ideas who challenges the status quo can invent a new product or service that might change the fortune of the company overnight. Similarly, a pessimist will be the first to address flaws in plans and designs, and the paranoid and aggressive employee who is very impatient will get work done without any delays. Therefore, it is essential to be tolerant of different personality types at the workplace and turn around any untoward situation or behavior at the workplace for the benefit of the employees and the company.

15 Toxic Employee Types

The Gossiper

You can choose your friends, but you can't pick your office colleagues. Therefore, adjusting to a new environment often turns out to be a difficult task. Many people are not very skilled in the art of persuasion, which is why they are left far behind and are alienated most of the time. A healthy work environment is necessary to increase employee productivity; therefore, maintenance of such an environment affects the work life of the employees.

"The gossip" is the most common problem people face at the office. This person is likely to talk behind people's backs and spread rumors. Rumors, an exaggerated version of the truth, greatly affect even people who say that they *"do not care for gossip."* Typically, employees who are new in an office are unaware of the work politics and find it difficult to adjust in their new environment. Such difficulties make the work environment toxic for people. Spreading rumors is quite easy but overcoming them turns into a nightmare for the victim. Gossip and rumors greatly influence the work environment as well as the relationships between employees and the bosses. At the same time, the victim of the gossip could be a gossiper too.

How can gossip affect the relationship between employees? Well, you would not want to talk to a person who greets you with a smile but talks ill about you behind your back. Often these difficulties are associated with moral values, since gossiping is ethically wrong and might result in several problems for the victim. The victim might start feeling alienated and isolate him or herself in the office. The victim might even stop asking for assistance from other colleagues, which can affect the work quality of the employee. The performance of the employee might start deteriorating with time; hence the entire work environment can be affected by a single gossiping mouth.

Once a woman in my friend's office spread a rumor about one colleague having an affair with her boss, who was 69 years old. The woman was only 29 years old, was happily married and had a beautiful daughter. She confronted the woman, and they got in a fight. The fight took a turn when the boss discovered the rumor and confronted the woman who started it. She was fired instantly for spreading the rumor. Thus, a single rumor destroyed her entire career as well as her reputation in the office. In the end, nobody gained anything from the situation, but everyone had an equal share in the loss associated with the rumor.

This problem might seem amusing to many people, but it can have a severe impact on the employee. From affecting their work life to their mental health, everything can be disturbed by the simple act of gossiping. Spreading rumors, especially if they are fabricated or untrue, can turn out to be the worst nightmare for an employee. Your team spirit can be ruined, and the work environment can become extremely toxic for other employees. Maintaining a balance between your work and personal life becomes extremely difficult in an environment where everyone is continuously interested in finding new topics for gossiping.

Anyone who is a victim of gossip remains the victim of gossip for a very long time. This also affects the firm's performance, since workers do not perform up to par. The skills of the employees are constantly challenged when they are continuously faced with people who do not appreciate their work. Unlike spreading rumors around the office, there are other types of gossip that can actually be good for the employee's career. Instead of focusing on the bad traits of a person, positive behaviors can be discussed to promote positive vibes in the office. We all have heard about karma, and some people believe in it strongly. Your positive behavior toward an employee might result in some kind of success for him/her, and you might be rewarded with the same good fortune further down your career path.

Character assassination and negative gossip is nothing but a waste of time that the employee could have used to enhance his/her performance. Remember, if a good deed is repaid, so are bad deeds. Instead of diagnosing the employees, supervisors and managers in small gossip sessions, the employees should utilize that time for enhancing their performance and lifting each other's morale. Employees must only be dedicated to their work, not to worrying about the personal lives of other employees.

You can avoid these situations by adopting a communication strategy for dealing with these employees. If you are affected, you should directly confront the employees who are spreading rumors about you. This can embarrass those employees as well as warn them for the future, and it can also develop an image of you as a strong victim who can effectively solve your problems. Moreover, you must not engage in any gossipy conversation in the office, and you must remain at arm's length from gossipy employees. The gossiper is only projecting his/her own insecurities by talking ill about other office mates. Therefore, the victim must avoid the gossip in the office and concentrate on setting a good example for others.

In the end, it is childish to think that gossip in the office can be controlled and its effects mitigated. As an employee, you need to focus on your performance and avoid the gossipers at all cost. There is no need to engage in activities that do not benefit you and waste your time by providing justification to every other person. The office is a place where you need to show your skills through your performance; therefore, you must clear your vision related to your future and focus on it. With a clear vision comes a successful career. Worrying about gossip will only hinder your career.

The Blamer

The environment at the office takes a new turn when there is a "blamer." This person creates another toxic layer in the office environment. Yes, these are employees who only know how to point fingers at other employees when the situation gets a little difficult to handle.

"Why didn't you prepare the presentation on time?"

"Oh, Mary asked me to help her with the report."

Is that even an excuse?

The example above can show what these blamers will actually do to shield themselves from criticism. They will go to any extent necessary to save themselves from trouble in the office. In short, blamers are the ones who invite the trouble and do not even accept that they were the ones who invited it. They are too stubborn to accept their mistake and apologize for it. Rather, they prepare their version of the story and shift the blame to whoever they see first (even the janitor. BEWARE).

The amount of effort and time they put into crafting their stories could be utilized to enhance their workplace performance. No matter what background these people come from, they are always the kind of people who suck the life out of you. They can easily turn your good day into a bad one, lower your sky-touching morale to the underground world where the elves live, turn a healthy person into a depressed alcoholic (in some cases), etc. Imagine the amount of venom these employees spill in the work environment to cover themselves from trouble. It becomes almost impossible to even breathe properly in an environment with such employees because their biting remarks always seem to spread like a poisonous gas in the air.

It might even be easier to deal with negative people than blamers because blamers are more toxic. They are a special kind of narcissist who ultimately believe that they can do no wrong. They think everything that happens around them or to them is because of other people. They will not waste a second to blame other people around them for anything bad that happens. They might even blame the people around them when they get asthma because they sucked in all the air.

Employees at the office who always find new ways to escape from difficult situations and save themselves from any trouble can often leave the other person depressed, stressed and feeling guilty for the deeds for which they are being blamed. The blamers rarely take responsibility for their bad performance or bad decisions. In the end, other employees have to suffer the consequences of the problems they created in an attempt to save themselves. They will try to put their ideas and suggestions above those of everyone else. They will continuously try to persuade their colleagues to accept their version of the story.

How does it affect the work environment? Well, it has a direct influence on the work environment. It creates a hostile atmosphere in the office and makes everyone feel reluctant. Other employees who are victimized by the blamers find it difficult to work on the same floor or even the same building as them. Moreover, the blamer is also left isolated by the other employees due to his habit of blame shifting. These people are extremely tough to work with, causing the work environment to shift from a healthy workplace to an unbearable hell. Now, the main question arises: How you can deal with such employees at the office?

As difficult as the question appears, the answer can be even more extensive and difficult. It requires the other employees to take extra precaution when dealing with the blamer in the office. Before initiating a new assignment with the blamer, you should make a clear effort to discuss every aspect of the assignment. You should discuss in detail the pros and cons of the assignment and also the responsibilities for each employee. This will help you develop a backup strategy to disarm the blame shifter.

Another useful technique to use against the blame shifter is taking responsibility for your mistakes as fast as possible so that the blame shifter cannot use it as a weapon against you. This will also help you develop a positive image in front of your boss and supervisors. By exhibiting such high standards, more employees will want to work with you. The dependence ratio can also increase on you due to your good moral behavior.

Even though the blame shifter can save himself/herself from trouble, the hostility that other employees develop toward them because of their actions cannot be mitigated. Therefore, just as performance and work quality are important in the working environment, taking responsibility for your mistakes and learning from them is equally important. By taking responsibility, you become aware of your weaknesses and use that knowledge to polish your skills and abilities. Those who feel too ashamed to admit their mistakes often lack some skills that are necessary for enhancing work quality.

In the end, shifting the blame on others always negatively affects the working environment and is ethically wrong. It can create problems for the blame shifter in terms of maintaining a positive and healthy relationship with other employees. Since all the employees work for the same firm and organization and continuously seek help from one another, it becomes important for the employees to promote positive vibes in the office. Taking responsibility for your actions and accepting your weaknesses always results in improving your skills. Thus, a positive environment can only prevail through the willingness of employees to develop a positive and healthy culture in the office.

The Flyer

The flyer is a no-holds-barred type of personality. The prominent behavior patterns of people with this personality type are excessive attention seeking, extremely emotional behavior patterns, persistent need for excitement, and an illogical and erratic cognitive style of functioning. Taking this a step further, other traits that these personality types exhibit are flamboyant and flashy theatricality in behavior, speech and actions. In addition, flyers use exaggeration to meet their emotional needs. Apart from this, they maintain a superficial and shallow relationship with their colleagues at work. When their needs are not met, it may lead to them getting very angry, blowing up and displaying their emotional histrionics. On the other hand, they may go to the other extreme and become very reclusive, quiet and depressed.

Flyers unsurprisingly gravitate to and settle in careers and workplaces that expose them to the applause and attention of an adoring fan mob or crowd. The professions that are best suited for them are the theater, politics, acting, and sales and marketing jobs in which they can satisfy their need for an audience when demonstrating and unraveling their theatrics. These personality types are quintessential "people persons." However, it must be noted that they are not overly intense, destructive, edgy and needy like psychotic personality types.

They have a very engaging demeanor and are very happy, persistently presenting themselves as genuinely likeable and amiable. It is relatively easy to be drawn to these personality types when they are in a pleasant mood. In typically subdued workplace settings and scenarios, they will be hugely entertaining, witty, energetic and funny. The flyer's light and humorous conversation is infectious. This behavior results in a pleasant change in stressful and hostile workplace situations.

One of the weaknesses that might affect the quality of a histrionic personality type's performance at work is their inability to make logical decisions. This feebleness is associated with their impressionistic cognitive style of functioning, both in formal and informal atmospheres. Most of their decisions are made on the basis of intuition and impressions. The flyer personality finds the rational and logical analysis of facts an invasive bother and annoyance. They just cannot be objective and detached when making a decision or a choice. It is almost impossible for them to think through a task logically when making a decision. Opinions and decisions in the workplace that are made emotionally and intuitively can have negative consequences.

For technology-reliant firms, these personality types may be hugely detrimental to the progress of the company. This is because these organizations require a high standard of technical excellence. Taking this a step further, all of the major projects for these companies require very accurate and detailed technical work procedures; very complex personnel management is essential in these organizations. These critical situations demand substantial, grounded and serious work and focus, and these work arenas call for and demand more than superficial theatrics and drama. Additionally, the flyer does not fit well in banks and financial organizations where number crunching and detailed analysis dominates most of the projects, and where there are routine, monotonous, isolated tasks. However, flyers can excel in careers that play to their strengths, such as advertising, human resources, sales and marketing, front-office, public relations, and customer relationships.

Before being too critical and judgmental about difficult personality types, it is wise to acknowledge their need for emoting and expressing their specific behaviors that are not particularly damaging. For example, the flyer personality needs appreciation and a little attention. These needs are not destructive and can be met by giving them an occasional pat on the back when they have contributed positively on a project or generally done a good job. Furthermore, when they need to make an announcement about their achievements, it's okay to spare some time and provide a listening ear and formally applaud their accomplishments. A neutral and logical way to deal with flyers is to try not to let their erratic mood swings affect you. Apart from this, when they get overly emotional or angry, make an attempt to stay composed and calm. Along with this, you should make an effort to quiet their restlessness and irritability. This can be done by settling them down in an isolated place, listening to what they are angry about and trying to reason with them.

Taking it a step further, having a supportive and honest conversation with these personality types is also very important. They must be able to get in touch with reality and realize what is happening. The realization that being overly emotional and dramatic at all times is not healthy both for themselves and the people around them is essential. They must eventually learn to control their flamboyant behavior, emotions and tendency to get angry and fly off the handle. However, in some instances these strategies might not work. During occurrences of extreme emotions and drama or extreme and erratic anger, it is best to safeguard oneself and one's interests. In these cases, the best thing to do is just accept that some behaviors cannot be changed. You need to either patiently deal with, or completely ignore, these behaviors and avoid any knee-jerk reactions.

Managers play an important role in dealing with difficult personalities, and they must take on the task of reinforcing positive, productive work-related behaviors among employees. The optimal way to deal with these personality types is to gently guide them into reality- and logic-based modes of thinking. Apart from this, instilling work practices that require attention to detail will assist in keeping them grounded and preventing them from resorting to theatrics and emotions. However, it is still wise to give flyers the attention and praise they need and provide them with an audience to whom they can voice their achievements. Taking this supportive approach and not completely isolating them with dull, tedious, pesky and detail-oriented tasks will result in a holistic individual with the right balance between emotion and logic.

The Work Shirker

Nobody gets paid to rest; everyone has to perform their part of the work. It's human nature to get tired of routine, day-to-day activities. However, that is no excuse; work shirking is not allowed. Work shirking can occur due to various reasons: laziness, distaste for work, fear, etc. In any condition, work shirking is beyond the ethical boundaries. It not only puts pressure on people who are already occupied in their work, but work shirkers also leave others with the burden of their work, yet they are the first in line when it comes to taking credit.

Some shirkers are clever and conceal their activities so artfully that it is almost impossible to recognize that they are shirking. It is necessary for everyone in the office to recognize when they are shirking and take measures to prevent this from happening from time to time. There are many ways a shirker may shirk work. For example, they may pretend that they are extremely busy when they are really only surfing the internet.

Shirkers are the most annoying personality at work. Everyone is frustrated by their continuous shirking and their everyday excuse of being "overloaded with work." They might be working on personal projects but pretend that they are engaged in the real work.

Their most irritating excuses are:

"Oh, I am already busy with the research project! Can you ask someone else?"

"This report will take a lot of time. I think it will take the entire shift."

"Sarah can do it better than I could ever do."

"If this project could be done by someone who has some insight into it, then it could be completed on time."

And many more...

What if the shirker has the authority to assign tasks? Simple: Your life is doomed.

The shirker will keep giving you the tasks he/she wants off his/her responsibility list. That means you will always be loaded with a lot of work. The shirker will set his/her target on you and completely destroy your life.

There are many ways to tackle such personalities in the workplace. First of all, recognizing this bad apple in the bunch is a necessary step. They have the tendency to justify even their worst decisions; therefore, persuasion skills are required to tackle them. If you have good communication skills, then you will be able to persuade such employees and fight back against their excuses. You and your other coworkers should not have to accept the burden of work from work shirkers. Everyone is busy performing their own tasks; therefore, it is unethical to unload your garbage onto others. You and your fellow employees should confront them on the spot and refuse to accept any assignments beyond your capacity.

The work shirker's attitude creates a hostile environment in the workplace and often leads to clashes among employees. Moreover, employees who are overloaded with extra work will generally make mistakes on a few assignments due to the pressure that has built up on them. All this is due to the laziness and unethical behavior of the work shirker. Simply firing them is not the best option to solve these problems except in extreme circumstances. Firing every other employee will develop a culture of fear in the workplace, which will restrict the employees from sharing their views with management. Instead, management should take measures to solve the matter as calmly and patiently as they can. Instead of saying *"You're fired"* try *"We need to talk."*

Apart from management, colleagues also need to play their part in solving the problem before it turns into a major dilemma. The employees can play their part by confronting the work shirker. However, the more important part to be played is by management. Management is responsible for assigning the tasks, and they are aware of the work load being assigned to each employee. They should take serious measures in order to teach the work shirker a lesson. Work shirkers damage the health environment of the workplace, which should not ever be accepted.

Management should take measures to assess the progress of their employees on a weekly basis. Several benefits must be granted to employees who perform well throughout the week. This will make the employees more enthusiastic about their work, and they will put in extra effort to perform well.

The sense of competing with other employees and the perks associated with the reward may even encourage the work shirker to make more of an effort. Thus, these measures can help maintain a healthy work environment. If the problem still persists, then management should take strict action against these people. Most likely, work shirkers will not care about these incentives due to their laziness and unwillingness to put in the work to achieve a better position at their job and earn other rewards.

The organization does not pay its employees to do nothing. If the employee is not performing as he/she is required to perform even after taking strict measures, then it is the duty of the management to remove them from the office. Their presence in the office not only affects performance but also has a severe impact on the work environment. Employees holding grudges against one another in the workplace is not conducive to the development of a healthy environment. The work shirker must not be given any chances to take advantage of other employees by convincing them to do their part of the work.

If the work shirker starts assigning the tasks to the employees, then he/she must be put under strict watch by supervisors to keep track of the work he/she does. Otherwise, this can lead to unequal distribution of tasks between employees and also create hostility between the employees and management. It affects the performance of the employees at the firm because everyone feels that they are not being rewarded justly. Therefore, extra attention must be given in order to maintain a healthy environment in the office, and critical measures must be taken to ensure the proper implementation of these measures.

The Competitor

Competition is very common in the workplace. Many employees are continuously engaged in beating their colleagues, whether in terms of salary or job position. Although it is necessary to maintain healthy competition in the workplace (otherwise the work environment turns into an ugly competition in no time) it is essential to differentiate between positive competition and positively awful competition. Many companies offer incentives to promote a healthy environment in the workplace; however, the competition often turns into a matter of life and death.

Employees typically experience one of two responses during competition: anxiety or excitement. If the competition causes anxiety in an employee, then that employee is more likely to engage in unethical activities to win the competition. However, if the competition causes excitement in an employee, then he/she might come up with a creative solution to the problem and win the competition. Moreover, if the competition is between two individuals, it can turn into a destructive competition and even give rise to hostility between them.

Here are some of the reactions you might notice during a competition:

"Hmm, I think the presentation should be more creative and contain all the necessary information in it."

"Why did he get a bonus even when I worked hard on the project?"

"We had a short deadline and not enough resources."

"Why do we have to do all the difficult tasks?"

"We had a greater work load than them."

Competition is a positive initiative that brings out the best in people; however, it can also create an unproductive and stressful environment. A competition helps employees to grow and learn a variety of skills, and it prepares them to accept the challenges being thrown at them in the workplace. It enables them to accept their defeats and learn from their mistakes. A competition also can bring out the creativity in a person and lead them to innovate new ideas, improving their performance.

Competition is intended to bring out the best in people; however, the situation gets worse when a competitor jumps into the situation with the sole aim of defeating his colleagues. Competition is about learning new skills by taking part in it, but some employees make it a matter of defending their honor. They want to win the competition by hook or by crook. This can affect employee productivity in the office. The competitors do not look at the competition as an opportunity to excel in what they are doing, and in this way, the intended goal behind the competition gets demolished.

Feeling challenged leads employees to perform better, but often they take the competition very seriously and destroy the fun behind it. Employees who do not treat competition appropriately generate a toxic environment in the office. These competitors often forget that they are competing with their colleagues.

Competitors easily get into fights with other employees and adopt strategies intended to hurt them. The essence of a healthy competition is employees competing against themselves. By competing against themselves, they may have a realistic chance of winning the competition, but they won't hurt anyone else in the process. No matter how tough the competition is, the employees should maintain order in the office.

For a competitor, acknowledgement and motivation from fellow workers is not enough. Such competitors usually pay attention to extrinsic rewards such as prestigious position, monetary compensation, extra perks, etc., instead of intrinsic rewards that come from self-satisfaction. For such employees, cheating is ethical in competition since they only look forward to winning the competition instead of using it to build strong ties with their colleagues.

Competitors who justly use the competition for their personal development and to learn new skills make the most out of it. Not everyone is blessed with every ability, and therefore everyone requires assistance at some point in life. Office life is no different; however, special skills may be required for you to achieve your goals. In the corporate world, skills develop over time, and colleagues are the first to help in developing those skills. No one will look forward to helping the competitor because he/she tends to have strained and unsatisfactory relationships with coworkers.

Instead of using the competition as a platform to earn material perks, you should always use it as a platform for personal development and building strong bonds with your colleagues. Making the most out of a competition is not a crime, but using unethical methods to achieve their goals is not a good option.

Employees can learn to implement new technologies, and the competition might even lead them to come up with creative ideas. Using unethical behaviors such as agreeing to help the colleague but planning to not follow through or taking credit for your colleague's work can create a hostile office environment.

It is essential for competitors to understand the true meaning of competition, and they must strive to maintain a healthy office environment. A competitor ruins the true essence of a competition by embedding negative vibes in it. Unethical measures taken by the employees can turn the competition into a nightmare for the organization. There are many ways to manage this type of behavior, but the initial step must be taken by fellow employees.

Competitors must not be given any attention and must always be avoided. Such employees intoxicate the environment and turn a fair competition into an unfair one. Their strategy to gain all the profits reduces the number of opportunities for other employees, which creates resentment in their hearts. The managers and supervisors must continuously change the criteria for winning in order to maintain balance in the workplace.

The Paranoid

The paranoid personality is often found in popular television shows and movies. This is because this type of personality is entertaining, quirky and frustrating, all at the same time. Most of these paranoid personality types have traits similar to people who suffer from paranoid personality disorder. Paranoid personality traits may range from idiosyncratic and unrealistic feelings of being persecuted, all in the complete absence of facts to support such vague feelings. These feelings result in a highly advanced and bizarre set of beliefs that are clearly delusional and false. Apart from this, they will always find the worst possible interpretation for anything anyone says or does, if it is associated with them. They have a heightened sensitivity to the words and actions of others. They also have a preoccupation and obsession with unjustified doubts about the trustworthiness and loyalty of associates, friends, family and strangers.

Most of their perceived slights from others' innocuous comments are blown out of proportion as signs of malevolent intentions and motives. Paranoid personality types have a persistent behavior pattern of suspicion and mistrust. Moreover, they tend to interpret and misconstrue other people's actions as malevolent, malicious, deceptive and persecutory. They have a general misperception that the world and its people are out to get them. Their level of distrust and cynicism borders on insanity and annoys anyone and everyone who is associated with them. Their perception of the world is so skewed that they think that people are mean, vile, hostile and selfish creatures. The world to them is a battlefield comprised of a sea of enemies in which they have to religiously keep their guard up and be alert and well-armed.

In a workplace scenario, they constantly are envious of the other employees and their bosses. Their incorrect view is that people in positions of power and authority naturally hate them because of their talent, intellect, experience and skill set. Taking this a notch further, they are obsessed with the wrong notion that their completely benign coworkers have a vicious motive to take them down a peg and demote them from their current position at work.

However, all is not gloom and doom; these quirky personality types can be brought to good, constructive use. Those with the paranoid personality type are capable of achieving considerable success at work in this highly competitive and aggressive global environment by being very combative against their very well-defined corporate enemies. They may also emerge as leaders in their pursuit of eliminating all the competitors who are scrooges in the war-torn world of corporations and oligarchs.

On the other hand, a battlefield and war zone mentality and outlook that is not kept in check by the paranoid personality type in the workplace can result in a negative upshot and effect. The vicious outward directed suspicion and mistrust that is always employed by the paranoid individual can blow back toward their subordinates and coworkers, causing devastation in their working relationship. This vile cycle of suspicion and hostility toward coworkers can result in the coworkers making every effort to avoid associating with them. This outright avoidance can be taken further, and the other employees may also resort to self-defensive moves. On the extreme end, paranoid personalities can harm their subordinates to achieve what they are pursuing. These rare occurrences may be caused by the incorrect thinking of these personality types that they are right to use any means necessary to safeguard what they feel they truly deserve from the unjust forces that are grouped against them.

Some of the character traits of paranoid personalities are being constantly suspicious of other people. The issue of trust always arises when dealing with these people. They generally interpret the behavior of others in negative and incorrect ways. The best way to deal with and communicate with the paranoid personality is to be very cautious when you speak to them and to recognize that your words may be taken in a different way than you intend. It is best to keep workplace assignments for people with this personality type straightforward and reasonable. Keep reiterating what you mean. Keep emphasizing that you meant well and that you did not have any ulterior motives or vicious intentions. Taking this one step further, also ask them to voice any doubts and concerns they have. Subsequently, make an effort to shatter any misgivings or apprehensions that they have by communicating that the work that has been assigned to them is free of any cruel intentions. However, if all your efforts to convince them that you are sincere and mean well do not bear fruit, just let go. Additionally, do not get caught up in changing and modifying their perceptions of people around them and the world in general.

Another way to deal with paranoid individuals is to put your foot down and provide upfront, non-confrontational but firm reality checks for their quirky misperceptions and misinterpretations. This approach must be used when the paranoid personality is not convinced by loose assurances and affirmations. This remedial measure must be employed in instances of considerable stress and anxiety, in which the conspiratorial and insidious cognition of the paranoid personality goes completely out of control. Another attempt at keeping their irrational attitude of suspicion under check is to engage them in projects that require minimal customer contact and team interaction. In such situations in which there is minimal emotional contact and little opportunity to distrust other people's intentions, these paranoid personalities will keep their eccentric thoughts to themselves, behave relatively normally and perform their work quite satisfactorily. When it comes to their interaction with management or their immediate boss, a manager can schedule periodic meetings to discuss organizational concerns and ongoing projects being designed by this personality type. These meetings can also serve as safe places for them to express their grievances confidentially and without any fear of reprisal. On the other hand, the managers must provide consistent and substantial reality checks with logical and firm explanations when faced with the paranoid personality's quirky behavior. These ways of dealing with and communicating with paranoid personality types can make life easier both for them personally and for coworkers and management collectively.

The Control Freak

The control freak is an absolute perfectionist who is extremely nit-picky and critical of himself/herself and others when executing a task either at home or in the office. This is due to the high and unrealistic expectations that control freaks or perfectionists have for themselves and others. These personality types have a tendency to be preoccupied and obsessed with control, perfection, over-analysis and orderliness. These controlling personality types are unable to function until they keep everyone and everything in perfect order. They are known for sticking to details and can be totally relied upon to carry out instructions to the letter. However, one disadvantage of being too concerned about the minute details is that they may miss the proverbial forest for the trees. In their effort to complete the task assigned to them with absolutely no errors, they might not be able to maintain deadlines and complete their tasks on time.

They exhibit many of the same character traits as individuals with obsessive-compulsive disorder. In an attempt to control situations, they do not mind stepping over healthy and pertinent boundaries. When these control freaks exhibit invasive, overbearing and annoying behaviors, it is wise to stay away from them and avoid interacting with them for a period of time. They are very uncomfortable with team projects and struggle with teamwork. They perform best in isolation and seclusion.

Due to their high attention to detail and rules, they are capable of being a valuable asset to the organization. However, they exhibit a controlling, inflexible and rigid behavior pattern. Control freaks are anxious about neatness, rules, perfection and orderliness. Apart from this, their intense rigidity can result in total preoccupation with lists, rules and details that might ultimately lead to panic disorders and persistent indecisiveness. People with a control freak personality type are overly committed to work at the expense of close relationships like family and friends. It is imperative that they avoid burnout to preserve their sanity.

These personality types excel in careers that require precision, perfection, accuracy and exactitude. Control freaks will never be annoyed and irritated by routine and monotonous work. They relish and enjoy the types of repetitive tasks that might numb the minds of many others. They have very high-level cognitive and logical skills and are best suited for jobs in the field of engineering, accounting and financing, banking, economics, and information technology. They are perfectly content in professions where they can be challenged intellectually and which require meticulous research. They make excellent scientists, planners, policy makers and employees of think tanks and universities.

On the other hand, they are complete misfits in professions that require the glib and witty adroitness of the flashy flyer and histrionic actor. They are not ideally suited for sales and marketing, advertising, public relations, or any profession that requires a flashy and flamboyant display of emotions, such as acting or theater. They are also much less likely to have flashes of insights and intuitive revelations that might prove beneficial for certain organizations. However, these personality types are not necessarily shy, like those with a quiet personality type. In situations that require them to display their social skills, they will make an earnest effort to put up a decent conversation and mingle with the crowd. However, their natural inclination is that they would rather be in the office, at their desk, than go for a quick lunch with colleagues or have a drink with a client.

Their narcissistic and flyer bosses can enjoy their parties while the control freak sits at his/her desk turning grandiose plans into workable and practical projects. At best, these obsessive-compulsive types get their job satisfaction from a job well done. However, at their worst, they are never satisfied with their work and become so anxious that they fear that there is no such thing as "good enough." They are prone to excessive worrying and overthinking. These obsessive-compulsive types also demand perfection for work in which perfection and exactness cannot be achieved. In such situations, they may brood to the point of negatively affecting their health. Taking this a step further, they may also drive everyone around them insane in their attempt to be perfect.

It is not easy task to deal with control freaks and communicate with them effectively. Ambiguity and non-clarity is what raises their anxiety levels. They are extremely uncomfortable with imprecision, mistakes and lack of clarity in work. When dealing with them, you must pay added attention and provide them with the complete details regarding the task that they have been delegated to accomplish. On the other hand, it is important to specify tasks that do not need detailed attention, in which it is not a sin to be less rigid and to take it easy.

It is also essential to emphasize that letting go of control at times, when the task or the situation does not call for it, is okay. Moreover, it is not the end of the world. Apart from this, in situations where their need for control is at its highest and their behavior is very rigid and inflexible, perhaps triggering an unwanted behavior from the respondents, it is best to stayaway. However, if staying away is not possible, then it is wise to not take their behavior personally. One more way to manage these personality types is to realize that they are not team-oriented folks. Taking this into consideration, it is best to permit them to work within their comfort zone, where they are able to control tasks that are within their territory rather than controlling and annoying other people around them. On the positive side, you need to make an attempt to pat them on the back or express appreciation for their attention to detail, due to which a project has been successful. All in all, taking the control freak's positive traits and accepting their phases of panic and anxiety is the ideal way to deal with them. Their perfectionism can be very advantageous for the progress of an organization.

The Pessimist

Moods are contagious, both at home and in the workplace, where many people spend 40 hours or more a week. A negative, pessimistic disposition can spread throughout the workplace, resulting in poor communication, reduced morale and less productivity. Employees and coworkers with a positive attitude have better communication skills. Apart from this, they spread a positive attitude around the office, which results in increased productivity and office morale. Pessimistic people foster a consistently negative and gloomy attitude in the workplace. These people typically expect the worst of situations and conditions. A negative pessimistic disposition in the workplace can create bad work habits that can adversely affect other coworkers. Pessimistic personalities types are generally very cynical, skeptical and negative. Their glass is never half full; it is always half empty. The behavior of these types of personalities can drag down the morale and confidence of other colleagues, dampening the morale of the entire workforce.

Negativity at the office spreads like wildfire. It can aggravate and embitter, ultimately killing the momentum of a team. Negative thinking can start to wear at efficiency in the workplace, leading to a lack of impetus and enthusiasm, a distracted and unclear mind, and a bad work ethic. An employee's wilting morale can have a damaging impact on the team and the productivity of the organization as a whole. Let us take a look at some examples of a pessimistic employee.

"This project is never going to make it."

Here, it is imperative for the boss to further question the fears and apprehensions of the pessimist.

"Why will the project not see the light of the day? What can we do to see it through to its completion?"

It is also beneficial to use and ask for alternative solutions by using the word *"but."*

"This project is never going to make it, but it won't do any harm to lay the groundwork and take the initial steps."

Though changing the attitude of a pessimist is a time-consuming and frustrating experience, it is important to direct and guide them consistently. It is beneficial to offer one's own productive criticism while providing a solution. Most importantly, it must be reiterated that energy and effort spent on negative attitudes can be redirected toward positive and productive activities.

It's vital to remember that the aim here is not to rid the team member of every cynical sentiment. Not all negativity is bad, despite how it sounds or feels. Some of the pessimist's concerns and skepticism may be relevant and rational. In addition, it may be based on a perception or insight that might be truly helpful to the team and could even save the company. A good example of this would be the infamous Space Shuttle Columbia fiasco. In this case, there were pessimists at NASA who didn't feel the Space Shuttle Columbia was ready, particularly after the Challenger disaster 17 years earlier. The Space Shuttle Columbia disintegrated upon reentering Earth's atmosphere, killing all seven crew members on February 1, 2003. After the Space Shuttle Challenger debacle in 1986, this tragedy was the second fatal accident in the space shuttle program. This exemplifies that not all pessimism is useless, unproductive and unsubstantial. Therefore, negative comments and statements must not go unaddressed.

Employees in the middle tier can also affect the workplace negatively. Their attitudes are problematic because they are never satisfied with the work of their coworkers or subordinates and consistently criticize other peoples' decisions. They are able to find faults and failings in almost everybody and everything. It is wise to deliberately stop yourself from getting dragged down by this personality type and believing all the negative feedback they usually give. Take, for instance, this example:

A senior manager gets some negative feedback from his client on a project that has been completed. He calls a meeting, and this is what he conveys to the pertinent team.

"The McCartney Project has been a total failure, a disaster story! This is what happens when work is not taken seriously and no one is committed. How will we retain this client and salvage the deal? We are doomed!"

To this doom and gloom narrative, a sensible team member could give a counter reply and make a concerted effort to lighten things up and make a point by responding:

"We can still salvage the project by making any alterations and modifications that are required and desired by the client. Perfection is a myth, and it's not like we haven't made an earnest effort and worked hard on the project. We can also schedule a meeting with the client to address any reservations that the customer has. Moreover, we as employees, value our clients too."

During the meeting, the employees need to just gather the patience to listen to the pessimistic boss vent out the rest of the disaster story. After the meeting, the employees need to objectively determine what needs to be modified and improved in the project, ignoring the exaggerated, non-substantive and pessimistic opinions of the cynic. Finally, the team must pay attention to how it might be able to improve the issue at hand and subsequently work on the project.

At the end of the day, it's tough to make an employee less difficult and problematic, but it is possible to learn how to deal with them more efficiently and smartly. By understanding these personality types and learning to identify them in your organization, you will arm yourself with the tools to get the most out of your employees, most importantly the difficult ones.

The Narcissistic Personality

The narcissistic personality type is a self-absorbed, self-indulgent, self-praising and self-loving individual with hardly a care about others living around him. He is vain, arrogant, haughty and difficult to deal with. He is consistently immersed in a behavior pattern that exhibits grandiosity, lack of empathy and a total sense of entitlement. Moreover, in narcissistic type personalities, there are exaggerated displays of self-confidence and a grandiose belief that they are the only ones who are highly accomplished and extremely talented. These personality types are commonly found within the higher echelons of conglomerates and corporations, particularly within the management levels of companies. They can more appropriately be described as egomaniacs or egotists with huge inflated egos and sense of self. They tend to evaluate their work performance very unrealistically and make exaggerated claims of achievements. Besides this, along with having inflated judgments of their own achievements, there is a counterintuitive behavior that they exhibit. It is their persistent underestimation and devaluation of the contribution of other employees in the workplace. In addition, they also have a tendency to be interpersonally exploitative. This is done by taking advantage of their employees to achieve their own ends and objectives. In a similar way, they have a complete lack of empathy and are unwilling to identify the feelings and needs of other people.

However, not all behavior of a narcissist is repulsive and grandiose. Some are simply innocuous and may also be healthy and essential for the workplace. Narcissism is a positive trait at moderate levels, as it positively affects self-esteem and confidence. A self-confident individual with a positive self-esteem is an ideal employee. His/her behavior is not only conducive for success, but he/she can be a source of inspiration for other employees as well. Apart from this, he can be a very good counsel and mentor for employees having problems with self-worth. Employees who are too insecure about their self-worth and are not confident enough perform relatively badly in the workplace. A narcissistic personality type can climb the career success ladder faster than other employees.

This is due to their extroverted nature, their general tendency to dream big and the belief that they can achieve great heights of success. They consistently seek fame, fortune and power, and their determination knows no bounds. They always believe that they are special and that they only deserve to socialize with special folks.

The most difficult task when dealing with narcissists is counseling or mentoring them. Their inflated egos and sense of entitlement causes them to be completely dismissive of any advice or guidance, even when there is a genuine need for improvement. A toxic narcissist is someone who thinks that his/her sense of entitlement gives him/her the veracity to exploit and manipulate other employees for his/her own vile purposes. These kinds of vicious personality types are usually found in the middle tier of corporations. They typically carve out their own little fiefdoms where they subjugate and repress their subordinates. In rare cases, narcissists at higher levels of management are also good at terrorizing their employees and being overly dominant of them. In these very rare and infrequent instances, corrupt, unfair and illegal practices are exposed and discovered during auditing for suspicious activities of the organization.

Narcissistic personality types usually try to gain support and control situations, to gather an audience to loudly proclaim their inflated view of themselves. It is a humongous task to ask or expect any improvements of these personality types because you cannot possibly improve on perfection. In cases where the narcissist realizes that others do not share his inflated sense of self, he will humbly forgive them for their short-sightedness and myopia. On the contrary and quite surprisingly, underneath the superficially bloated egos of these narcissistic personality types lies a very fragile sense of self-esteem and apprehension about their self-image. Most of their deep-seated insecurity issues arise from their persistent need for appreciation.

Some of the character traits of narcissists can be molded for their benefit and that of others around them. It is wise to consider flattery and stroking their ego when they do a job well and when another job needs to get done. An interesting associated character trait of the narcissistic personality is that he/she can feel very degraded, insulted, humiliated and haunted by even very minor criticism in the workplace. Therefore, the wise thing to do when conveying bad news or providing constructive criticism is to offer a little praise and compliment them for an earlier accomplishment. Then, gradually convey the criticism without being vile and vicious. Finally, end the conversation on a pleasant note. This dialogue is a good example:

"Hey Donna, good going with the Telecom project. You certainly are taking your team to great heights. It seriously shows!"

"However, let's be realistic and get down to the nitty gritty and get our hands dirty. The clients required detailed and appropriate designing for some application development tasks. Are you getting that, pal?"

Finally, the concluding pat in the back with a gentle reminder:

"I trust your team to make the perfect revisions and come out as winners again. I just know that because you are leading the team!"

However, in instances in which they have really put in the effort and truly deserve the applause and appreciation, take the opportunity to give them their due and then praise them openly, either by taking them out for a drink along with the rest of the team or stating their achievement in chain emails sent out to all the employees. This will prove to be very effective in continuing to get excellent results from them in the near future.

All in all, it is not right to have major expectations from individuals with difficult personality in every situation. It is wise to maintain realistic expectations and hopes and be patient and tolerant. When narcissistic employees bring forth nonsensical, unrealistic and self-aggrandizing plots and ideas, do not pay any attention and just walk away without wasting any more time. However, not all of their insights are vague, pie-in-the-sky ideas. Some of them might be substantial and logical, and these ideas and insights must be taken seriously. If the narcissistic personality is dealt with diplomatically and wisely, his/her best character traits will shine and be beneficial both to himself/herself and the organization as a whole.

The Hisser

A hisser is as unpredictable as a snake. You never know when or how hissers will attack. A snake does not attack unless it is provoked in some way; the same is true of a hisser personality at the office. Usually hissers do not react, but when they do, they either rant, whine or rave. They are extremely pushy people and are often bullies.

Such employees are difficult to change, and therefore managers should consider getting rid of them. The situation can be difficult to overcome since these employees act unpredictably when provoked. They might be funny at times, but anything can provoke them.

Hisser:

"Look at your hair! So greasy! Hahaha!"

Other employee:

"Where did you get your tie? Did you borrow it from a clown?"

And suddenly the entire situation has changed from being funny to potentially violent.

It is tough to predict the mood of a hisser, and thus, staff members need to pay extra attention to protect themselves from the wrath of such an individual. Often anger leads people to do things that are harmful to them and others. People sometimes behave like children when they are extremely angry. For instance, they do things without thinking about the consequences.

The first step in dealing with such people is that they must be looked at as children. Some people are difficult to change, but firing them should not be your first option. Although it is not the responsibility of management to take action to help the person get better, it is necessary for management to take steps to facilitate treatment for such employees and create a healthy environment. If management only looked for perfect employees, they would not find anyone to work for their firm. Aside from management, the colleagues of such employees can also play an important part in maintaining a healthy relationship with these employees.

Saying "No offense" before telling a joke might reduce the likelihood of the joke being taken negatively. If someone does not tend to take jokes well, then other employees should be extra careful around him/her.

The simple philosophy of "If you can't endure, then do not initiate" must be put into action. If you can't handle the potential response, don't make the joke.

The behavior of the hisser is sometimes due to bitter past experiences or because they might be overloaded with work, which makes them pissed off at everyone else. Putting yourself in someone else's shoes can help you understand the situation that the other person might be going through. Even though privacy must be maintained at the workplace, if the behavior of the hisser remains persistent and if he/she looks disturbed most of the time, then there is nothing wrong with asking for the reason behind their antisocial behavior. The basic aim behind every measure taken by the firm is to ensure a healthy environment in the workplace. Thus, the employees should settle their disputes and try to maintain a sound and healthy workplace. Moreover, if a situation takes a serious turn, then proper evaluation of the matter is necessary before taking any strict measures against any employee. Although hissers are difficult to handle and have low patience levels, they are still not always responsible for the bad things that happen in the workplace. The blame should not automatically be put upon the hisser as soon as the situation gets a little out of hand.

Management should be well aware of the situation of their employees and must hire them after passing them through the proper channels. Such behaviors can be detected at the initial stage of screening by taking several measures in the start, but if somehow the strategy does not work out, then the employees must try to make adjustments to deal with such individuals.

There is no point in discussing the person with one another; however, the employees can directly confront the employee and ask him/her to change his/her behavior a little bit. By talking to the hisser directly, the employees can develop a fair and reliable relationship with the hisser. There are many other steps the employees can take in order to develop a strong relationship with the hisser.

It might be difficult for other employees to deal with such difficult personalities at the office, but that does not mean that other employees should avoid them and ignore them due to their behavior, since both the hisser and the other employees need to make an effort in order to mitigate the effect of a hostile environment at the office.

In the end, although someone with a hisser personality might be difficult to deal with, he/she must not be ignored due to his/her behavior. Management and the employees must take initiative to deal with the hisser in a viable way in order to develop a healthy working relationship among employees. However, if none of this works out with such employees, then the other employees should maintain their distance with them as much as possible.

A workplace needs to have a healthy relationship among employees. The only way to establish such a relationship is by accepting the flaws of other employees and dealing with them accordingly. Therefore, it is the duty of every other employee to treat their coworkers with respect and without generalizing. Avoid gossiping behind each other's backs and stop spreading rumors about each other. A hisser is a difficult personality; however, it is not impossible to deal with. Thus, to keep the environment healthy, everyone should play their part.

The Einstein Type

From electrical energy and automobiles to medicine and satellites, innovation has made the world better. The information technology revolution has made the world more productive and advanced. Apart from this, global economies are driven by innovative industries that are constantly evolving to meet the needs of a changing world we live in. Innovations, and the subsequent revolutions, are the result of both the provision of government funds in basic research and private-sector ingenuity and investments. From the advances that put a laptop on every desk and a smartphone in every hand to the discoveries that led to life-saving vaccines, all major innovations are thanks to the efforts and the originality of Einstein type geniuses. Two major examples of Einstein type personalities are Steve Jobs and Bill Gates. As an employee, Steve Jobs wasn't a favorite of either his team at work or his bosses. Consequently, the first thing he did when he became the CEO of Apple was to encourage and drive employees to voice their ideas and, more importantly, to put them into practice. Organizations find it extremely difficult to be convinced by the visionary's ideas and tend to be dismissive regarding them. It was Steve Jobs who vehemently supported creative culture in the workplace. He believed that every organization needs to be run by ideas and not by hierarchy. Furthermore, he emphasized that the best idea must win, not the best person with the most seniority and power. Everyone within a company has something to contribute to that company's progress, and great ideas do not necessarily come from the senior hierarchy of companies.

A workplace environment is not just about the usual sales talk and the pep talk that an HR manager gives to the employees in an organization. It is about the nitty-gritty work that comes with grandiose ideas that managers spin in board rooms, and it is about bringing pie in the sky ideas to fruition. Subsequently, thinkers need doers to implement their ideas. Managers and the upper hierarchy in organizations need nonconforming voices to check their assumptions and push their ideas. Einstein type personalities fit the bill and are very different from most people in the world. They are individualistic and extremely curious and inquiring. They are unique individuals who do not come a dime a dozen, hence the expression "*You are no Einstein*," commonly heard in workplace settings. There's nothing these people would dislike more than being "*one of the crowd.*" Their curiosity compels them to get to the bottom of things and to understand everything around them. They hate to be stuck in monotonous, repetitive and routine work. They are preoccupied and obsessed with concepts and principles and are always in pursuit of the universal law behind everything they see. They want to investigate the unifying composition of life in all its intricacies.

The Einstein types are earnestly of the opinion that the unexamined life is not worth living. Their ingenuity and creativity knows no bounds. Organizations have been contributing substantial sums of money to research and development, and Einstein types fit perfectly in these business units. Their unique perspective and vigorous intellect makes them perfect for one-person jobs, and they make natural mathematicians, system analysts, philosophers, architects or professors. Just as their personality type suggests, they have been responsible for many scientific discoveries throughout history. Their unrelenting imagination, open-mindedness and creativity are not tools of some quest for emotional validation and to spread a dogma. Since they are not people-centric, small, technical workplaces and fields such as crime investigations, forensics, law and laboratory research are ideal careers for Einstein personalities. Most often, investigative and fact-finding professions involve working with ideas and require an extensive amount of thinking. These occupations involve figuring out problems and searching for the facts that Einstein type personalities excel in.

The Einstein types are not always boring nerds, and are even sometimes innovative enough to make the workplace more entertaining than it usually is. They are the office revolutionaries who can actually teach you how to make your workplace fun, unlike traditional workplaces. An Einstein employee will always come up with new and innovative ideas. Their sense of humor might not be so strong, but their sense of arranging and managing things beats every other employee in the office. These geniuses are always looking for new ideas to utilize things in the office with their unconventional creativity.

However, all these strengths do not come without a set of weaknesses. Einstein types are quite shy in social situations. More intricate situations such as social and business meetings aggravate and annoy them. In a similar vein, their family and close friends struggle to get into their hearts and minds. Furthermore, they remain so open to new information that they often never commit to a decision at all. This applies to their own skills as well. These personality types know that they improve as they work on a project and that any work they do is second-best to what they could do. Unable to settle for less due to their high professional standards, the implementation or completion of their task is sometimes delayed, resulting in losses for the business.

They are eccentric, extremely logical, solitary and independent, and these character traits are not always conducive or desirable in business environments. It can be extremely difficult for these personality types to secure a job, and they sometimes struggle to find careers that meet their requirements. This does not mean that they remain unemployed. They possess qualities that have a much higher demand in specific industries, and these qualities are an innovative spirit, a passion for applying theoretical and scientific approaches and ideas, and creativity. However, to harmoniously blend into an organization, the Einstein type has to make an effort to be more social and not isolate himself/herself. Additionally, he/she has to learn to do tasks that are less creative and imaginative. If Einstein type personalities are able to put their best foot forward to secure a position in an appropriate job, they will prove to be very beneficial to the organization they serve.

The Victim

Apart from many other roles that an employee assumes in an office, being a victim is the role many employees are ready to assume to receive sympathy from other employees. There are two types of victim employees, one who embraces the role for the rest of their lives and another who embraces the role for a shorter period of time. The difference between these two types of victims is that the former does not learn from their experiences while the latter does learn from the experiences and moves on. Turning into a victim is completely in the hands of the individual; however, some employees indulge in self-victimization out of habit.

An employee indulges in self-victimization to control the feelings, actions and thoughts of other people. Other reasons include to seek attention, to justify the abuse of other people and to cope with difficult situations. These reasons are only excuses to satisfy one's need without asking for it. Playing victim is easy in a work environment, but most often it is driven by personal desires and needs. The victim's mentality is quite different from that of the other employees working in the workplace. The victim will always seek to achieve his goals and needs by adopting the strategy of self-victimization, whereas most employees seek to achieve their goals through hard work.

Employees who are continuously involved in self-victimization often lack self-confidence, which is why they search for easy ways to achieve their goal. The most common type of victim is the person who complains a lot! These types of employees are extremely annoying and are constantly complaining about their salary, job, etc. Over time, the other staff members start ignoring the person due to their constant whining. People start avoiding him/her in day-to-day activities, such as at lunch, at hangouts, etc.

No one can be saved from the wrath of a person who self-victimizes. Although they usually appear innocent, they tend to be jealous of almost every coworker in the office. When an employee receives a promotion or any kind of praise from their supervisor, the victim will be the first to start finding errors in their decision. Jealousy is not healthy and beneficial in the work environment, and the person who gets jealous is usually concentrating on the weaknesses that make him/her insecure. It is necessary for employees to support each other and feel happy for each other's success. There is no person on Earth who is perfect; thus, we all learn from one another.

Moreover, a person inflicted with the disease of self-victimization is often found pitying himself/herself. Most of the time, the victim will create situations so that other employees sympathize and empathize with the victim. This strategy further alienates them within the workplace. Moreover, the employee mentions old grievances to appear as a victimized person, thus continuously creating situations to receive sympathy from other employees.

The victim employee often lacks assertiveness, which is one reason why they use the strategy of passiveness and submissiveness. This strategy often deteriorates their self-esteem and personal development. A person who is involved in self-victimization in the office often finds it difficult to trust other employees. This is because the victimized person does not believe in his/her abilities and does not trust himself/herself. Their actual insecurities result in lack of trust in themselves, which frequently affects their performance at work. Moreover, the lack of trust can also isolate them in the office since they do not trust anyone with their work.

The person in the office who is frequently involved in self-victimization cares too much about the perceptions of other people. The victim is continuously involved in trying to improve his/her habits and personality, not for the sake of improving performance but to satisfy other people. His/her work quality and performance continuously suffers setbacks due to continuous efforts to make everyone else happy instead of himself/herself. Despite these continuous efforts, the victim fails to impress those who pass judgment on them. As a result, they are extra sensitive to every judgment being passed on them, suffering depression and anxiety in several phases of life.

Every situation in life offers an opportunity to bring out the victim in us and turn the situation in our favor, but being a victim does not help us grow. When a person is in the corporate world, it is necessary for him/her to learn every day. Learning is a part of life, and it must continue to improve performance and work quality. It is essential for people to understand their situations and learn from them. Every difficulty is a lesson that is only learned by bravely dealing with the situation; therefore, people should avoid victimizing themselves either in the corporate world or in their personal lives.

In the end, it can be concluded that self-victimization is the weapon of a coward who is scared of accepting his/her weaknesses. No matter how intense or difficult the situation gets, you should never use self-victimization for the realization of your dreams. However, in an office where everyone is striving to achieve a better position, those who self-victimize often steal several opportunities from their coworkers. This ends up destroying the relationships between those employees and their coworkers. Keeping the work environment safe from toxic people is often difficult to achieve, and self-victimization of such employees worsens the situation. Maintaining healthy relationships is necessary in the corporate world since everyone is connected to every other person and everyone is continuously engaged in asking for assistance from one another.

The Psychopath

Before considering your colleague a normal person, you need to take a look at the checklist, which will help you identify the psychopath in your office:

- Manipulatively charming
- A "BURN THEM ALL" attitude
- A chameleon
- A hot-headed freak
- Does not show many emotions
- Lack of remorse
- Thrill seeker
- Stays away from responsibilities
- Egocentric

Did this help you identify the psychopath in your office? Well, this checklist is just a starter pack of the whole package that comes with the psychopath. Imagine seeing a guy who looks no different from any other person but is planning to kill his boss in his head. Well, a psychopath is much more than that and equally toxic for the environment in the office.

Let's start with his/her manipulatively charming behavior and attitude. The psychopath will almost always have a smile on his/her face, greet everyone with a hug, engage in entertaining conversations and always be ready for a comeback. Don't be so inspired by his attitude; it's just the first stage of psychopathy. Everything that comes with an "extra," be it extra cheese, extra spice or extra charming, is not good for anyone's health. Therefore, whenever you spot an extra charming boss or employee at the office, try to decode that smile on his/her face, and your smile will be lost forever.

"BURN THEM ALL" does not necessarily mean setting the office on fire, but it could be not far off. As normal as the psychopath may seem, he/she might be involved in criminal and illegal behavior. Other employees might not realize it right away, but they will soon realize that they cannot trust the psychopath with anything. BEWARE!

Chameleons are cute, but psychopaths are NOT! They change their colors faster than they change their clothes. These individuals are skilled at masking their emotions and are masters of playing dumb. They change their persona quite frequently in order to impress other people in the firm or company, especially the boss or those who are above them in the company. The statements of these individuals cannot be trusted as they change them like a chameleon changes his colors. Can you see the resemblance between these individuals and chameleons? Don't take your chances with them.

If you want to confirm whether an individual is a psychopath or not, try to insult him/her. A psychopath will lose his/her head and turn into a *WhatsApp* emoji. The psychopath can never overcome even petty insults at the office. Everything that happens to him/her turns into a matter of honor. They are aggressive and overly sensitive to slights or insults. Most people in the office are prone to responding calmly to the insults, but that is not the case with a psychopath. The seemingly friendly psychopath at the office is not so friendly after all.

As tough as the psychopath looks from the outside, he/she also has a heart of stone. It is impossible for the psychopath to feel empathetic or sympathetic toward other employees. The word "feeling" has no definition in the psychopath's dictionary, only "I," "me" and "myself." It is completely normal for the psychopath to express no emotions, no matter what happens. If you closely examine their impressions, you will realize that they are either masking their true emotions or they genuinely don't care about anything. If this explanation reminds you of anyone at the office, then you are probably dealing with a psychopath.

The psychopath will show no concern about the effects that his actions have on other people in the office. Psychopaths are too stubborn to realize that they did something wrong and are continuously trying to rationalize their behavior. They will find excuses to cover their actions and, in some cases, they completely deny that they even did something. The lack of guilt and their ability to rationalize their emotions is what makes their personality even worse.

Thrill seeking is fine, but seeking thrills like a psychopath is completely unacceptable. They see crime and other illegal activities as thrilling or exciting. They are often adrenaline junkies who are willing to do anything in the name of thrill and excitement. They are easily bored with their day-to-day routine and tasks and are looking for something new for their excitement.

They don't take responsibility for their work and completing their tasks on time. Psychopaths do not care about obligations or commitments. They rarely come through on their promises.

What is a psychopath if not egocentric? Ego is of great importance to the psychopath. They see themselves as the center of the universe, and therefore, whatever they do can never be wrong. The rules and regulations they have formulated for themselves are of the utmost importance, and everything else does not matter. The psychopath is arrogant enough to deceitfully impose his opinions and rules upon others and control their lives according to his/her plans.

A psychopath may have a lavish life, a great position at the office and many people respecting him/her, but that might not be enough to please him/her. Psychopaths have grandiose personal visions for themselves because most of the time their thoughts are overshadowed by the fake personality they have developed for themselves. A psychopath might be successful but have no one to celebrate his/her success with. The other employees mostly feel resentment towards them, and are often reluctant to develop stronger bonds with them at the office due to their cunning behavior. Therefore, psychopaths must try to maintain a positive relationship with everyone in the office to develop a healthy working environment. Psychopaths must engage in activities with other employees in order to develop strong bonds with them.

The Quiet Type

Typically, employees fill the silence with loud words in an attempt to look like the smartest person in the room. Meanwhile, some people sit in the corner observing everything. In some cases, these are the actual smartest people in the room. On the other hand, their silence can simply be due to shyness. Generally, those who stay quiet and observe everything going around them benefit more than those who stay quiet due to shyness.

Shyness is not considered acceptable in the corporate world since everyone wants to impose their presence on others. When employees wear the mask of shyness, they seldom make their presence felt in the office. Meetings are conducted so that employees can put their ideas forward in front of their supervisors and bosses. If an employee does not take advantage of that time, he/she will soon be ignored forever.

Most of the time, such employees fear being misinterpreted or of not being able to express their idea properly in official meetings. Speaking in front of a group of people increases their anxiety levels, and they often end up ruining the entire opportunity. It is essential for these employees to overcome their fear of failure and anxiousness in order to deliver their thoughts to the others in the office. They need to develop more confidence in themselves and use such opportunities to polish their communication skills.

A person who develops a habit of being persistently quiet must choose a career that fits with their strengths. For example, a shy employee should avoid jobs that involve continuous persuasion through words or speech, such as sales jobs. Candidates who are quiet and shy should adopt careers in fields such as writing and research so that they are comfortable and do not feel the pressure to take on an entirely different persona.

Now the question arises: How can a quiet person develop relationships with colleagues?

It is very difficult to communicate with these individuals because most of the time, their answer is either *"yes"* or *"okay!"*

One woman in our office gets scolded by our boss all the time. Why? Because she does not have the ability to speak up for herself. She accepts whatever is thrown at her, even if she has no idea how to do it.

It is important for these employees to demonstrate their contribution in the workplace so that everyone is aware of their presence. Although they are quiet, management can still get them to contribute to office practices through various means. They may not be as vocal as others, but they definitely have ideas that need to be heard. They can utilize emails or a close friend in the office to convey their thoughts and ideas to other employees or to the organization. Moreover, proactive responses and recommendations can also help them develop a bond with their colleagues.

Other employees in the office often consider the quiet employee to be irrelevant due to his/her lack of interest in office politics and discussions. The other employees develop a perception of the quiet employee that can turn into a nightmare for him/her. It can mitigate their chances of getting leadership opportunities and preferential job assignments. It is necessary for quieter employees to seek new opportunities that give them the center stage. Moreover, all employees should avoid creating a culture of developing perceptions of and assumptions about every other employee in the office.

The quiet person might be shy, but most of the time he/she is considered to be the humble leader at the office. They are honored and recognized as people who often help others at the office. They are recognized as people who bring some great qualities to the table for other employees. For instance, they have strong listening skills, analytical skills, etc. Their attentive listening skills enable them to critically analyze a situation and brainstorm more appropriately when they work alone. Thus, these employees can prove to be beneficial in problem-solving and can easily negotiate difficult situations. Moreover, these employees are typically considered trustworthy and discreet.

The ability to maintain a quiet composure in the office helps the employee build a reputation for self-contained and reflective professionalism with other employees. Any sensitive information regarding the firm is safe with these employees, and they don't usually engage in office politics, which makes them appear trustworthy. Therefore, many of their colleagues consult them in matters where protecting sensitive information is required. They must be assigned to tasks that require strong listening and analytical skills.

It can become quite difficult to deal with such employees in the office. They often don't speak about the difficulties they are facing in the office or don't ask for help due to their shyness. Other staff members ignore them because of their apparent lack of interest in most workplace situations. This can cause them to develop severe depression since they do not feel they can speak about anything. There is a good chance that they will miss all the opportunities that come their way.

These individuals can turn out to be talented employees who can greatly benefit the organization. They need to work on their persona in order to increase their productivity at the office. They do not need to pretend to be an extroverted person to mask their shyness. However, perception plays an important role in corporate life and can often result in the employer and fellow employees developing a permanent image of the person. This perception can shape the employer's view of that employees working performance and can also destroy the corporate profile of the employee.

In the end, being a shy person is not a crime, but when you are in the corporate world, you need to speak up for yourself. Being quiet can often lead to missed opportunities, and it can also affect workplace dynamics.

The Instigator

The workplace can turn into a toxic environment if it is home to an instigator. It is very important to properly handle any interactions with this person. There are various ways in which an instigator can stir up conflicts and bad blood between individuals. These individuals use tactics such as drama, gossip, negativity or anger to achieve what they want. The instigator always has a "Charlie Chaplin" look on his face and is always looking forward to creating drama. They will greet you with a smile and try to gain personal information, and then they will use that information against you.

"Hey Andrew! How are you? Wow, you look so happy these days! Did you know that Christine dyed her hair red again? She looks so ugly with it!"

Meanwhile, Andrew is thinking about who Christine in the office would be.

"You know what, Stephanie? Elizabeth told me that she thinks you are not qualified for your job and that you look so pale and lazy all the time. She even said "Who would even hire her?!" I mean Stephanie, no offense, but that girl just doesn't like you. Stay away from her."

Mission accomplished for the instigator!

How can this behavior even benefit anyone, even the instigator? What kind of satisfaction can anyone achieve by turning people against one another? Only an instigator can answer this question!

Well, you can't do much if an instigator is present in your office, but you surely can ignore these people and save yourself from their wrath.

First, avoid interaction with them! They are not people anyone would want to be friends with. If they speak ill about other people in front of you, then they can also talk ill about you behind your back! Beware of these people at all costs. Avoiding them does not necessarily mean that you actively stay away from them in the office. Rather, just avoid interacting with them on a personal basis.

Second, remain calm and don't let them win by upsetting you. Instigators are always looking for ways to upset people; therefore, their conversations must be waved off with a "yes" or "okay." By engaging yourself in conversation with the instigator, you will only dig a hole for yourself.

Third, reply with positivity. Wear a bright shining smile on your face to keep their negativity out of your way. This is the best way to deal with such employees in the workplace, and it will also create distance between you and them. When they see that you are not interested in the drama, they will stop coming to you. Hence, ignorance is bliss.

Fourth, if the issue remains persistent and the instigator starts interfering with your work and private life, then speak to management about it. If the instigator is violating any company policies, then it is your duty to involve management rather than dealing with the issue on your own. This way, your other colleagues will also be made aware of the instigator, and it will also serve as a warning for them.

Need more advice as to how to handle instigators at the office?

Tell them what you want, but don't explain it to them. Rather, order them to do it: "It should be done the way I told you to do it!"

- ❖ Never allow them to take the reins.
- ❖ Ignore their conversations: "Oh sure! I will let you know." (But never let them know.)
- ❖ Don't make them the leaders; make them followers.
- ❖ Criticize their work quantity and question their resiliency.
- ❖ Tell them that they are wrong and not working up to par.
- ❖ Be extra nice with them so they are even more pissed.
- ❖ Question their strategies and methods! This will infuriate them more.

Some precautions:

Your private life is not a joke; therefore, you should protect your personal life at all costs. Do not share your personal information with everyone in the office. Choose your friends wisely and don't start sharing sensitive information with them just after befriending them. At the end of the day, privacy is critical.

Warn the boss about such people at the office so they are aware of their tactics beforehand. Use every strategy to guard yourself against them. They can even cost you your job; therefore, take extra measures to counter them before it's too late.

Stay calm no matter what happens. Keep yourself at peace when dealing with difficult people. If you are exhausted or annoyed, there is a fair chance that they will keep attacking you from time to time. But, since these people are always looking for drama, if you don't provide them with it and act unbothered, then they will stop coming back to you.

Make things easier for yourself and take measures to protect yourself from the wrath of these people. Clear the air behind closed doors and confront them at the initial stage. Don't let them play games with you, and don't give them the opportunity to place you in a bad light. Don't confront them in front of other colleagues because it can make you look like the bad guy. These people are masters at utilizing situations for their own benefit. Beware!

These instigators also do not shy away from controversial topics. Criticizing or questioning other people's religious beliefs is one of their favorite pastimes. Therefore, avoid such individuals at all costs and do not befriend them. They are not even loyal to those who help them in their most difficult times; they are only looking for gossip and drama. Befriending an instigator has never helped anyone, and it never will.

5 Toxic Bosses

The Inexperienced Boss

Generalizations and assumptions are common in the workplace, both by employees and bosses. It becomes quite difficult to support your boss, avoid generalizations and maintain a healthy working relationship if your boss is inexperienced. Moreover, the other employees will take such individuals very lightly and not listen to them since they see them as untested. This type of behavior from the employees destroys the employee-boss relationship and often ruins the work environment.

The best way to deal with inexperienced bosses is by listening to what they have to say with an open mind. Pre-assumption and hypersensitive behavior from employees makes them insensitive toward their boss. The appropriate mindset is, "Although the boss is inexperienced, he is still our boss, and it is our responsibility to treat him/her with respect." He/she is the boss for a reason and deserves the respect and support of the employees. A healthy working relationship is difficult to establish, considering the barriers between a boss and the employees. Pre-assumption and generalization deteriorate this relationship to a much greater extent.

Every boss has been inexperienced at some point; therefore, it is only a matter of time before an inexperienced boss becomes an experienced boss. The employees can act as a resource and help the boss learn things quickly, even though inexperienced bosses may not be able to offer direction and make correct decisions.

It's a common belief that *"People don't leave firms; they leave bosses."*

However, this is the best time for employees to play a leadership role. A lot of employees find it difficult to deal with difficult and incompetent bosses, and they quit their jobs. Instead, they should try to deal with the parameters their bosses create for them instead of searching for new jobs.

Often the feeling of hostility is partially due to pain and jealousy because their boss got a promotion before them, which makes it difficult for them to hold their tongues. Therefore, these employees sometimes use harsh and sarcastic language in order to belittle their boss:

"Your idea is good, but I think you are too incompetent to properly handle that task."

"Well, I think we should seek an expert's advice on that issue."

And more...

These employees only dig a hole for themselves by getting involved in a direct conflict with their bosses. The employees need to focus on their job and the leadership role they can play from within. Even if a manager lacks expertise in a certain area, another employee can take charge and help the inexperienced manager learn about the challenging circumstances.

A jealous employee will always focus on the problem and will never help the boss. However, other employees take charge and help the new boss adjust in the new environment. This not only helps the boss but also the employees in the office who might be affected by his poor decisions in the near future.

Instead of focusing on the problem, you should learn to focus on the solution. If your new boss is not making the right decisions, then ask him the right questions in order to guide the situation in the right direction.

Even bad managers have some redeeming qualities. Try to analyze those good qualities because they will partially overshadow the bad qualities and lead you to develop a healthy relationship with your boss.

NEVER gossip about your manager to others in the office. No matter how bad your manager may be in some areas, sharing your negative feelings with other employees is never the best option.

Never make the mistake of discussing how you feel about your manager with your colleagues. You can never trust anyone in your office, plus it will restrict your manager from growing into the role of experienced manager.

Even though you might help your manager learn new things, it still does not make you responsible for the bad decisions that he makes. Help your boss, but never cover for him/her, since it does not help anyone. No matter how much you try to help, it never fill the gaps that are left by their deficiencies.

"No, that's not how it is done. You were wrong!"

"Sorry, but it was you who told me to move those files from there!"

"You told me that the deal would not benefit us, which is why we dropped the idea."

Be straight forward, even if you are working under a strict or incompetent boss. There's a fair chance that he might not know when to hire and fire people. You can be the hero and make everyone's life in the office easier.

Moreover, keep in mind that helping can be a risky tactic when dealing with your boss. Some bosses are abusive, and some are generally calm and understanding. Never try to push the limits with your boss, no matter how much you help them.

The Invisible Boss

The invisible boss! As frustrating as the name sounds, these personalities are even more frustrating. When you do something good, it is because of your boss's leadership, and when you do something wrong, it is your fault. These double standards are what makes these the most annoying bosses. They can usually be found wasting their money like a pro or taking vacations on exotic beaches. They are professional blame shifters, but will be the first to collect the rewards.

These bosses are difficult to handle since most of the time they are not present at the office, and when they are, they are usually pissed off at everyone. Their invisibility is the reason for the unhealthy environment at the office. When the manager is not present at the office, how are you supposed to deal with difficult situations? Who is going to provide you with expert advice? Who will guide you when something goes wrong?

A manager is an important asset in the office, which is why he/she is always loaded with a lot of work. It's the boss's responsibility to take care of matters at the office rather than wasting his/her time on some beach. When it comes to taking responsibility and guiding the employees, he/she must be there.

However, such individuals are difficult to handle since they do it on purpose, and the employees cannot directly communicate their weaknesses to them due to the communication barrier. So, how are the employees supposed to deal with them?

Well, it is both a refreshing and a frustrating feeling for employees when their manager is not present at the office. It is refreshing because they don't have to deal with the manager's tantrums all day, and it is frustrating because when something goes wrong, it all becomes your fault. Thus, maintaining a good relationship with the manager benefits the employees in every aspect. Who knows? The manager might become impressed with you and make you the interim manager to deal with difficult situations at the office when they are not there.

Such bosses will leave you wondering where they are and how they would react to your work on a project. You might think you are doing things the right way, but your boss loses his temper when he/she looks at your work. This puts double pressure on the employees. They might have to do the same work multiple times due to a lack of guidance from the manager.

This not only ruins the work quality and performance of the employees but also makes them resentful toward their bosses. Thus, a time comes when the employees are no longer capable of handling this situation and quit their job. The firm suffers at the hands of an invisible boss. The employees don't perform up to expectations and thus, become frustrated with their work life. By doing work beyond their capacity, their health also starts deteriorating.

How ironic it is that an invisible person can affect so many lives in the office. Now, how do you handle the invisible boss?

When your boss treats you like you have the plague, do not react by wondering *"What did I do?"* Instead, take a deep breath and try to answer as calmly as you can, sounding unbothered by the question. Your calmness will show the boss that you have actually spent time on your project and that you are understand the work. Playing mind games with your boss is not an easy task.

Next, try to collect as much information as you can when your boss is present at the office. Completing a task on your own might be difficult for you to handle since you are not fully aware of your boss's mentality. Therefore, before you start working on a project, try to communicate about it with your boss more often so that he/she is well aware of your performance. Finally, don't be too submissive. Even if your boss is aggressive and cannot hold back from abusive remarks, never change your values for him/her. There are a lot of other jobs available, and you surely can find a better boss. Speak up for yourself so that your boss knows that there are employees working in his/her office, and not puppets.

If you are being blamed for something that is not your fault, use your voice, but do not sound threatening, since your boss always has plenty of options to replace you. Never take chances, and don't let your frustration at the situation get the best of you because you could put your job at risk.

No matter how difficult it becomes to deal with your boss, still make an effort to develop a strong, healthy relationship with him/her. When it comes to dealing with your boss, each and every employee should play his/her own part. Learn about your boss's patterns and try to deal with him/her accordingly. This will save you from going against him/her and also mitigate the potential risks of dealing with your boss. Try to communicate your problems with your boss and show him/her that the boss is a crucial part of the office. This strategy might remind the boss of his/her importance in the office. Also discuss your concerns regarding his/her constant absence from the office. By taking small steps and measures, employees can develop strong ties with their boss. Your invisible boss is still your boss and has the power to replace you. If the situation gets out of hand and your integrity is being challenged, then resigning is the only alternative left for you.

Micromanager

How do you deal with a micromanager without killing yourself? These types of bosses observe you so closely that you feel eyes staring at you even when you are sleeping. Micromanagers ruin the atmosphere for everyone in the office. They always have an excuse for their excessive supervision, such as:

"They will mess up things if not supervised properly."

Yeah, we understand but supervise us without killing us!

Most employees quit their jobs due to their boss, not because of the salary or even the job itself. While the invisible boss doesn't care at all, the micromanager cares way too much.

These bosses behave like they know everything, which leaves the employee frustrated at the micromanager. The employee might have more experience than the manager, but he/she will still criticize all of the employee's decisions and strategies. The employee does not have the choice of questioning their boss. Rather, he/she is forced to accept whatever the boss throws at them.

"My boss thinks he knows everything. He's always criticizing my work and telling me what to do. I cannot bear this anymore. Do you have any recommendations?"

"He thinks he is the boss, so he can do anything. Who gave him the right to destroy our lives like this?"

"Ignore him. I think he has been ditched by too many people. That's why he wants to control everyone in the office."

These are some examples of the comments you will hear from employees regarding their micromanager bosses. No one wants to be controlled, and the work environment needs to be friendly in order to maximize productivity and work quality.

There are many possible reasons why these micromanagers treat their employees the way they treat them. It may be due to insecurity, the fact that they are high performers themselves, neurotic tendencies.

Even the micromanager's smile upsets employees sometimes because of the micromanager's scrutinizing eyes and *"I-want-it-perfect"* behavior towards his employees.

Now, the question comes, how can you dodge those eyes?

In short, live and let live. Defer and let them do your work. Just as bosses use their employees to win, it's your turn to use your boss to win. Thank them frequently for guiding you and showing you how things are done. Mission successful!

Don't increase your boss's expectation level. If you act dumb and show that you only know enough to survive in an office, then your micromanager will gradually accept your lower standards. Keep your manager under this assumption so that when you perform well, he/she will think *"Oh wow! Sam is performing so well"* and will eventually leave you alone. You can also perform well without your micromanager constantly checking on your work, and you can prove this to your manager through this strategy. Moreover, the micromanager might be treating you so badly because he/she has nothing to do. Try to keep your boss busy through various means so that he/she is unable to micromanage you anymore. Distract them by giving them something else to do. If your micromanager is not busy, then he/she will bug you over every little detail. If you don't want to ruin your performance, take action. Furthermore, try to anticipate whatever they do. A micromanager is probably a micromanager at home too. These types of people may have OCD and can't do anything without worrying. They worry excessively; therefore, being an employee, it's your responsibility to update your micromanager from time to time regarding sensitive and important tasks. This technique will help the micromanager to control his/her anxiety and will also reduce the micromanager's level of interference with your work.

Micromanagers are like zombies in *"The Walking Dead."* They can be cured, but it requires a lot of time, patience and understanding. Thus, the employees must put extra effort into helping their micromanager boss if they want a career at the firm. The manager should always be there to help you, but excessive interference can ruin the work completely. This behavior from a boss can also create mistrust between employees and boss.

A good boss will recognize the strengths of his/her employees. He/she will put them in the best possible position where their strengths can be utilized. A good boss will check on you once in a while to see if you need any help. Such managers are respected by all of the employees in the office. Also, they promote a healthy working environment in the office. It is important for the bosses to be lenient toward their employees, but not too lenient, in order to maintain the boundaries between the employees and the boss.

Even when they put these measures in place, dealing with micromanagers is extremely difficult for employees since their experience and integrity are constantly being questioned by the boss.

Negative Boss

Next up are negative bosses who do not know how to treat their employees as human beings. Instead, they treat them like assets or resources. They are the type of bosses who are negative, focused on numbers and self-centered. A negative employee can be taught, but if the boss is the one spreading negative energy around the office, then it becomes difficult to deal with. Employees in this situation feel that their only choice is to accept what their boss asks them to do, no matter how difficult it is for them.

Why are such negative bosses allowed in the office when negative employees are generally thrown out of the office after a certain amount of time? Maybe they brought in a big client for the organization, their parents hold stock in the firm or they are otherwise qualified for the job. Whatever the case may be, they create problems for employees that can only be treated by becoming submissive toward the negative boss.

In an ideal world, everyone would have a fantastic boss who helps them grow and succeed, stands with them, takes blame for them when appropriate, and is a team player. Then again, that's in an ideal world! In the real world, dealing with a negative boss might become a nightmare for the employee.

The negative boss might criticize everything you do, from your clothes to the cover page of your report; nothing is safe from them. You might think that you have created a masterpiece, but they will definitely not like it. They will always pinpoint the negative aspects and never encourage employees for their positive traits. Negative bosses usually focus on the numbers, metrics and analyzing problems. Such bosses frequently insult their employees verbally. This type of behavior makes the employees loses their confidence and leave them feeling undervalued.

So the question is: How can employees deal with such bosses in the office?

It can be difficult to deal with negative bosses at work, but employees should develop strategies to deal with them in order to maintain their position at the workplace.

Speak up for yourself!

Never settle for less, and never undermine yourself because your boss is negative and can't praise you for your good work. If he has been criticizing, you for a long time, then it is time for you to stand up for yourself and tell your boss that you have put in extra work on the project.

Identify your boss's motivation. What drives him/her? What makes him/her angry? What makes him/her so critical? What is it that annoys him/her? By identifying these drivers, the employees can use them against the negative boss. What if he/she doesn't care about how much time you spent on your lunch, but instead he/she cares about how other employees might look at it? These drivers are the essential tools in employees developing a strong bond with their negative boss. You cannot directly control your boss's negative behavior, but you can use indirect strategies to control the effects of this negative behavior on employees.

Next, don't let it affect your work. If you are aware of the uncontrollable nature of your boss's behavior, then don't pay attention to it. Even if you pay attention to it, it will not solve the problem for you; therefore, it is better for employees not to pay heed to the negativity of their boss. Another strategy to deal with such bosses is by staying one step ahead of your boss. If your boss asks you to deliver something, then reply *"I already put a draft of the document on your table."* If you stay one step ahead, your boss will stop throwing negative comments your way and will also develop a positive impression of you. Moreover, set boundaries. Don't tolerate an insult or attack if you don't deserve it. If your boss insults you without boundaries, then you need to speak up and show that you are not going to tolerate it.

Although bosses have all the power in the office, that does not mean that they can spread their negativity as much as they like. *"Good fences make good neighbors"* should be followed religiously with your boss and other supervisors who try to sabotage your integrity. Stop assuming that they know everything and that only they can help you when you are faced with a problem. Stop going to them for every little thing and try to solve the problem on your own. Their managerial title does not mean they have all the right answers. This type of behavior by employees makes managers and supervisors believe that they are extraordinary and that nothing can be done without them.

Take responsibility and act like a leader in front of the negative boss who is always looking for excuses to insult you. If you know the right direction for your firm, then go ahead and take charge. However, don't undermine your boss; keep him/her in the loop. You surely don't want to lose your job! Avoiding your boss and his/her decisions is not the solution. However, there are many indirect strategies that can help you block out your boss's negativity. Keeping it simple, don't cross your line, and don't let your boss cross their line. Even if you are an employee, you are in that position because you have the desired skills and because you are the best!

Don't accept everything your boss tells you. Fight for your rights when you need to, and quit if your boss don't change his/her behavior with you.

The Workaholic Boss

Work is essential for our well-being, identity and sense of self. However, there is a substantial difference between working hard enough to live a balanced life and being a workaholic. It is essential to know the difference between the hard worker and the workaholic. A hard worker maintains a healthy balance between work and personal obligations, unlike a workaholic. A hard worker is present for his/her family members and friends. Hard workers do not let work hijack their personal lives. Any added time at work to meet deadlines is balanced by maintaining a decent schedule after the erratic work calendar by the hardworking employee. On the other hand, a workaholic manager or boss lacks the good sense and wisdom of a normal hardworking employee or boss. They are obsessed with their work and addicted on the adrenaline high it gives them. They just can't seem to get enough of work, and this applies both to themselves and their coworkers. They stay late at the office, check their email at all hours and even put in time on the weekend. Furthermore, they expect their employees to do the same.

Workaholism is a soul-shattering compulsion that changes people's personality and the values they live by. It threatens family security and often leads to family problems. Unfortunately, workaholics eventually suffer the loss of both personal and professional integrity. Workaholic bosses have their coworkers reach one goal and immediately set another more ambitious one for them. For a workaholic, staying at the same level of accomplishment is considered a failure. Some employees of a workaholic boss are complacent and submissive. These coworkers will do what the workaholic boss wants them to do. They will stay late at work, ignore their personal needs and family, and work on weekends too. However, other employees may be wiser and more assertive and may set boundaries. This does not mean that they will not complete the tasks given to them by the stated deadline.

You do not have to have a job to be a workaholic. Many obsessive homemakers and students suffer from this condition as well. If your manager is a workaholic and works crazy hours, do you have to also? No, you do not! You need to set the right expectations and boundaries. It is unwise to compare the amount of work an employee of a workaholic does with that of his boss. Workaholic bosses place unreasonable and unrealistic demands on their staff, which can lead to breakdowns in both physical and psychological health.

A healthy conversation with a workaholic boss who has expressly criticized you about your working hours or availability, can go like this:

"There were two deadlines back to back. You were nowhere to be seen last evening"

"Why do I need to stay late at work? I will be done with these tasks before the end of the day today. That is my responsibility: to ensure that I do my job well and on time."

Moreover, it is imperative to set healthy boundaries that let you attain both your professional goals and your other life goals. When an employee is asked to work overtime on a project multiple days in a row, the employee must ask for a lighter work schedule after the difficult project has been completed. When employees are expected to always be on call, these unrealistic demands must be countered wisely. You need to speak up and assert yourself in such situations to save yourself from overwork. This conversation can go something along these lines:

"I am doing a reasonably good job, and I intend to continue to do a good job, but I am not available to answer the phone after a certain time."

When these sensitive issues are being discussed, it is crucial to be careful about timing. Getting into delicate conversations when the boss is extremely worked up about the task at hand is foolish and self-defeating. It is important to pick an appropriate time when trying to explain to a workaholic boss that overworking is not going to be productive in the long run for you as an employee. Do this by stating your need for working decent hours in terms of a long-term benefit to you, your boss and the organization as a whole. You could explain this by saying:

"Having some quality time to myself or with my family is an indispensable part of my life; it is very important to help me avoid burnout and exhaustion."

Thankfully, not all workaholic bosses expect their employees to have the same insane work ethic and follow the same work schedule as they do. If the boss is sending emails at 4 am, it does not mean that he/she expects you to read it at the same time and start working on the task. Some workaholics just like to get things out of the way and get all information out as soon as possible. They like to delegate tasks to the pertinent employees ahead of time.

After making all of these adjustments when dealing with a workaholic boss, if things still do not improve, all you can do is to accept the fact that your boss cannot be changed. You need to just come to terms with the fact that you and your boss have dramatically different ideas about work-life balance. Stay the course with balancing the amount of time and energy you should be devoting to your job with the amount of time you want to spend with family and friends. It's perfectly okay if the gap cannot be bridged. Most importantly, employees must not let the anxiety of the workaholic boss affect them. They must remain composed, centered and not absorb the negative energy around them.

Toxic personalities as assets in the workplace

No workplace is complete without the negative, nagging, unkind or super-competitive people who make other employees' work life hell. The wisest thing to do is learn how to deal with toxic people in the workplace without risking your own success. You cannot just stay away and alienate yourself from those critical, fault-finding, negative, rude, gossipy, conniving or otherwise toxic personalities in the workplace. You need to cooperate and coexist with them on some level and utilize their negative and positive traits for the objectives of the organization.

You cannot escape these people; they're part of your everyday routine. Toxic people may undermine, cause disruption or sabotage; whatever their treacherous actions and motives, they do have an effect on the people who have to work with them. We have deeply explored toxic personalities and how to deal with and managing them. However, the most effective approach is to use some of their seemingly negative traits for the larger benefit of the organization.

Control freaks can be extremely annoying with their nitpicking, over-analysis and orderliness. However, due to their attention to detail and concern about rules, they may prove to be a valuable asset to the organization. These personality types shine in projects that require accuracy, exactitude, precision and perfection. In the same way, though most narcissists have inflated egos and sense of self, not all of the narcissist's behavior is grandiose, exaggerated and repulsive. Narcissism is a positive trait at moderate levels because it positively affects self-esteem and confidence. An ideal employee is a self-confident individual with a positive self-esteem. A narcissist can be used as a mentor in the workplace who counsels employees who are having problems with self-worth. Apart from this, he/she can be a source of inspiration for other employees as well.

Paranoid personality types are capable of achieving considerable success at work in this highly competitive and aggressive global environment, where no organization has good intentions regarding their competition. This is because they can be very combative against their very well-defined corporate competitors. Similarly, pessimistic personalities can be life savers. Not all pessimism is useless, unproductive and unsubstantial. A good illustration of this is the infamous Space Shuttle Columbia fiasco.

Flyers can never get enough of histrionics and loud displays of emotions. However, no organization can do without these lively and bright individuals. They are the life of every organization. Additionally, without them there would be no entertainment industry. There would be no *"woods,"* such as Hollywood and Bollywood, and no theater.

In the same way, we would be living in ancient times if not for the Einstein types of the world. There wouldn't be a laptop on every desk and a smartphone in every hand. Furthermore, longevity and good health would just be a far-fetched dream.

The concept of healthy competition is solely based on bringing out the best in people. Competitors don't always jump into the situation with the exclusive aim of defeating and overpowering their colleagues. Some competitive employees do not make it a matter of honor or a matter of life and death. They do not participate in competitions to win them by hook or by crook. They participate in them to do their best and put their best foot forward to achieve the objectives of their organization. Competing and feeling challenged to excel leads employees to perform better. Competition is also about competing against yourself and pushing yourself to do the best you can. It includes self-grooming and teaching yourself added skills that might be fruitful in the workplace.

Gossipers can be encouraged to mingle in more productive and positive ways. This can be done by encouraging them to be emphatic and to engage with their colleagues in a less damaging way. But these very difficult personality types must also be dealt with firmly. In a nutshell, it is frivolous to think that gossip in the office can be controlled and its effects can be mitigated. Gossipers who do not show signs of improvement must be taken to task for the overall benefit of the employees and the company in general. Employees' private lives are not a joke or a gossip story to spread around; therefore, you should protect your privacy at all costs.

Employees must be forewarned not to share their personal information with anyone in the office, particularly with the gossipers. A similar type of problematic personality is the instigators. They live for drama, gossip and chaos in the workplace. They also need to be treated with a firm hand and be consistently monitored and directed to work on their weaknesses.

On the other extreme of personality types is the work shirker. This lazy and inept personality constantly requires bosses or colleagues to wake him/her up so they can smell the coffee. These people can be best dealt with by having them adhere to strict deadlines consistently. It must also be noted that their excuses should not be accepted. On the other hand, those with victim personalities must also be controlled. You should never be complacent with them or offer them empathy or sympathy. Intermittent reality checks must be made by reminding them to own up and take care of their responsibilities. Finally, the most difficult of the personality types, the psychopath, must be convinced to get professional help.

Conclusion

Toxic behavior arises principally from the high load of stress many people carry in the modern world. Some of the reasons for this stress are the rise in global competition that has compelled organizations to operate tightly, a decline in free time, multitasking and other work pressures. The absolute best way to counter negative, toxic and annoying people is to surround yourself with people who lift you up and give you positive energy. Make a conscious decision to spend more time with the exciting, happy, positive and constructive people in your workplace. Happy and balanced people are a great counterbalance to toxicity and bad behavior.

If you are a sole proprietor, you can control your own behavior. However, in big organizations in which standing teams and project-based collaborations are the standard, bridging differences takes substantial effort. General difficulties in communication, minor disagreements and misunderstandings are a common workplace feature, but dogged and prevalent regular stresses are perilous for the long-term stability and productivity of employees at the workplace. Despite the ill effects of surviving in these toxic environments, employees usually endure these workplace situations since their livelihood is on the line. It is their source of revenue and their only means of supporting themselves and their families. Conversely, in such situations, toxic colleagues have more opportunities to create chaos and destruction. Furthermore, in workplaces where employees are targets of verbal abuse, criticism, bullying and other types of viciousness, eventually their morale evaporates, job satisfaction declines and their engagement in work diminishes.

If you cannot physically move on to a new position or a new company, it is imperative that you mentally move past toxic people. Leave them behind or keep a safe distance from them. If they are not helping you and are only being a negative influence, they don't deserve your attention. You have power over them. There is a famous adage from First Lady Eleanor Roosevelt that *"No one can make you feel inferior without your consent."* This cannot be truer!

You have no control over other people's behavior, but you can certainly control your response and your reaction to them. Don't let negative personality types infringe on your peace of mind and sense of sanity. Sometimes, setting boundaries and putting your foot down can also do wonders. It is good to create boundaries by defining what behavior is acceptable. See that you clearly communicate these boundaries to the people you have created the for.

The wisest option is to control your reactivity, regulate your emotions and send out a clear message to your toxic coworker or boss. Here's where you have the most leverage. Most fundamentally, stay logical, to the point and objective. Be assertive and say no to demands that feel unreasonable, without justifying or defending yourself. This can be achieved by having a few good mantras on hand so you can deliver them on time and when you need them most:

In instances when a toxic individual blames you:

"You have to stop passing the buck and own it. I will not accept the blame because I am not at fault."

In the event that someone is bullying you:

"I'm not going to continue this conversation if you're going to call me names."

Or on occasions when the toxic personality has totally lost it:

"I'm happy to discuss this with you when you're calm."

Let's also mention the top-tier bosses of organizations and their toxic behaviors. Although the easy way out when you are dealing with an extremely bad boss is to pursue other employment, this isn't always possible or even a wise step to take. The senior hierarchy and management are supposed have real leaders guiding and motivating their subordinates and the teams that they manage. Real leaders and bosses don't seek to criticize for the sake of criticism. If they criticize, it's meant to help you grow, not tear you down. This is known as constructive and healthy criticism. Real leaders don't belittle and demean their employees. Bosses aren't dictators. However, in some cases, they abuse their position of power. If an employee is feeling manipulated, abused, overwhelmed, dominated and consistently criticized, it's because they are not dealing with a real leader; they are dealing with a severely insecure individual who is on a power trip. Instead of creating a work culture where everyone can thrive, this person has created a toxic work environment that causes havoc both to the employees and the organization as a whole. When toxic behavior takes hold of an environment, it turns everyone cynical.

No matter how hard it gets in a non-conducive environment, there is still a chance to maintain sanity by being balanced and objective, and not taking things personally. In addition, do not compromise on your values, morals and convictions just because toxic personalities are on an eternal war path. Making an earnest effort to maintain your integrity and keep your head up high is a prudent thing to do when confronted by toxic personalities. At the same time, maintain an excellent rapport with colleagues and bosses, and exhibit healthy behaviors in your circle of influence.

It's sad but true, life isn't a cake walk, and it also is not fair and reasonable. You might have to occasionally encounter or work alongside toxic people throughout your entire career. This book has made an effort to investigate toxic personalities, both among the employees and the bosses of organizations. In addition, it has tried to provide alternatives in dealing with them and managing them accordingly. The book suggests looking at the situation from a more positive and constructive perspective. This is done by projecting and utilizing the problematic character traits of these difficult personalities in channels and tasks at which they excel so they can be productive members of their organizations. All in all, the book explains different ways to constructively and effectively deal with toxic personality types to help both the employees and boss sustain a healthy professional life.

One last thing

If you enjoyed this book or found it useful I'd be very grateful if you'd post a short review on Amazon. Your support really does make a difference and I read all the reviews personally, so I can get your feedback and make this book even better.

THANKS AGAIN FOR YOUR SUPPORT!

Please send me your feedback at

susan.howard.usa@gmail.com

www.ingramcontent.com/pod-product-compliance
Lightning Source LLC
Chambersburg PA
CBHW070304220526
45465CB00004B/1736